Day Hike!

SPOKANE
COEUR D'ALENE
& SANDPOINT

Day Hike!

SPOKANE
COEUR D'ALENE
& SANDPOINT

Seabury Blair Jr.

SASQUATCH BOOKS
SEATTLE

Printed in China

Sasquatch Books with colophon is a registered trademark of Penguin Random House LLC

24 23 22 21 20   9 8 7 6 5 4 3 2

Editor: Gary Luke | Production editor: Em Gale
Cover photograph: Kim Kozlowski | Cover design: Hilary Grant
Interior photographs: Seabury Blair Jr. | Interior design: Andrew Fuller
Interior composition: Liana Lewis | Maps: Marlene Blair
Copyeditor: Rachelle Longé McGhee

Library of Congress Cataloging-in-Publication Data
Names: Blair, Seabury, author.
Title: Day hike! : Spokane, Coeur d'Alene, and Sandpoint / Seabury Blair Jr.
Description: Seattle, WA : Sasquatch Books, 2018. | Includes bibliographical references
    and index.
Identifiers: LCCN 2017041446 | ISBN 9781632171146 (paperback)
Subjects: LCSH: Hiking—Washington (State)—Spokane Region—Guidebooks. | Hiking—
    Idaho—Coeur d'Alene Region—Guidebooks. | Hiking—Idaho—Sandpoint Region—
    Guidebooks. | Spokane Region (Wash.)—Guidebooks. | Coeur d'Alene Region
    (Idaho)—Guidebooks. | Sandpoint Region (Idaho)—Guidebooks. | BISAC: TRAVEL /
    United States / West / Pacific (AK, CA, HI, NV, OR, WA). | SPORTS & RECREATION /
    Hiking. | TRAVEL / Special Interest / Sports.
Classification: LCC GV199.42.W22 S645 2018 | DDC 796.5109797/772—dc23
LC record available at https://lccn.loc.gov/2017041446

ISBN: 978-1-63217-114-6

IMPORTANT NOTE: Please use common sense. No guidebook can act as a substitute for
experience, careful planning, the right equipment, and appropriate training. There is
inherent danger in all the activities described in this book, and readers must assume full
responsibility for their own actions and safety. Changing or unfavorable conditions in
weather, roads, trails, snow, waterways, and so forth cannot be anticipated by the author
or publisher, but should be considered by any outdoor participants. The author and publisher will not be responsible for the safety of users of this guide.

Given the potential for changes to hiking rules and regulations post-publication, please
check ahead for updates on contact information, parking passes, and camping permits.

Sasquatch Books | 1904 Third Avenue, Suite 710 | Seattle, WA 98101
SasquatchBooks.com

CONTENTS

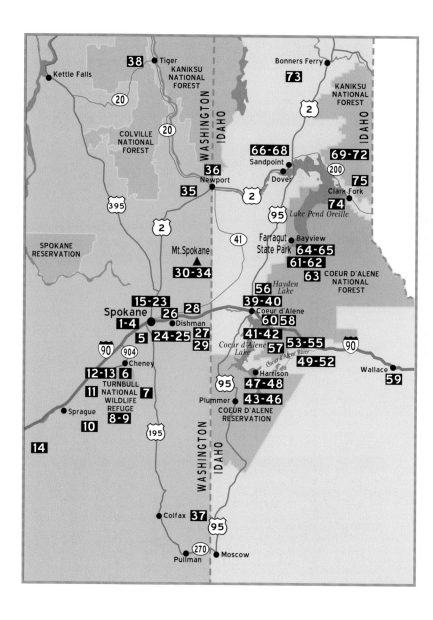

HIKES AT A GLANCE

EASY

NO.	HIKE NAME	RATING	BEST MONTHS	KIDS	DOGS
3.	South Hill Parks Loop	★ ★ ★ ★	Mar–Nov	✔	✔
9.	Bluebird Trail	★ ★ ★	Apr–Oct	✔	✔
13.	Fishtrap Lake	★ ★	Apr–May, Sept–Oct	✔	✔
18.	Indian Painted Rocks	★ ★	Mar–Nov	✔	✔
21.	Spokane House	★ ★	May–Sep	✔	✔
30.	Hay Ridge Loop	★ ★ ★	Jun–Oct	✔	✔
39.	Tubbs Hill Loop	★ ★ ★ ★	Mar–Oct	✔	✔
43.	Lakeshore Loop, Heyburn State Park	★ ★ ★	Apr–Sep	✔	✔
47.	Trail of the Coeur d'Alenes, Harrison–Sqwe'mu'lmkhw	★ ★ ★	Year-round	✔	✔
50.	Trail of the Coeur d'Alenes, Medimont–Lane	★ ★	Apr–Oct	✔	✔
51.	Trail of the Coeur d'Alenes, Bull Run–Black Rock	★ ★	Mar–Oct	✔	✔
53.	Trail of the Coeur d'Alenes, Cataldo–River Bend	★ ★	Mar–May, Sep–Oct	✔	✔
55.	Trail of the Coeur d'Alenes, Pine Creek–Gap Rock	★ ★ ★	Mar–May, Sep–Oct	✔	✔
66.	Sandpoint Long Bridge	★ ★ ★ ★	Year-round	✔	✔
67.	Pend d'Oreille Bay Trail	★ ★ ★ ★	Year-round	✔	✔

MODERATE

NO.	HIKE NAME	RATING	BEST MONTHS	KIDS	DOGS
1.	Downtown River Walk	★ ★ ★	Mar–Oct	✔	✔
2.	Fish Lake Trail	★ ★ ★	Apr–Oct	✔	✔
4.	South Hill Bluff	★ ★	Apr–Oct	✔	✔
5.	Columbia Plateau Trail, Fish Lake–Cheney	★ ★ ★ ★	Apr–Oct	✔	✔
6.	Columbia Plateau Trail, Cheney –Long Lake	★ ★ ★ ★	Apr–May, Sep–Oct	✔	✔
7.	Slavin Lake	★ ★	Apr–Oct	✔	✔

No.	Hike Name	Rating	Best Months	Kids	Dogs
8.	Stubblefield Lake Loop	★★★★	Apr–Oct	✔	✔
10.	Columbia Plateau Trail, Downs Lake North	★★	Apr–May, Sep–Oct	✔	✔
11.	Columbia Plateau Trail, Amber Lake North	★★★	Apr–May, Sep–Oct	✔	✔
12.	Hog Lake	★★★	Apr–May, Sep–Oct	✔	✔
15.	Palisades Park	★★	Apr–Oct	✔	✔
17.	Bowl and Pitcher Upriver	★★★★	Apr–Oct	✔	✔
22.	Milepost Zero	★★★	Mar–Nov	✔	✔
26.	Beacon Hill	★	Apr–May, Sep–Oct	✔	✔
35.	Pend Oreille County Park	★★	May–Sep	✔	✔
38.	Frater Lake	★★★	Jun–Sep	✔	✔
40.	Tubbs Hill Summit	★★★★	Mar–Sep	✔	✔
46.	Trail of the Coeur d'Alenes, Plummer Point–Hndarep	★★	Apr–Oct	✔	✔
49.	Trail of the Coeur d'Alenes, Medimont–Gray's Meadow	★★★★	Apr–Oct	✔	✔
52.	Trail of the Coeur d'Alenes, Bull Run–River Bend	★★★★	Mar–Oct	✔	✔
54.	Trail of the Coeur d'Alenes, Cataldo–Enaville	★★★★★	Apr–Oct	✔	✔
56.	English Point Loops	★★	Apr–Jun, Sep–Oct	✔	✔
57.	Fourth of July Loop	★★★	Jun–Oct	✔	✔
61.	Farragut State Park, Beaver–Buttonhook Bay Loops	★★★★	Jun–Sep	✔	✔
62.	Farragut State Park, Willow Lakeview–Buggy Trail Loops	★★	May–Sep	✔	✔
64.	Mineral Point	★★★	May–Sep	✔	✔

MODERATELY DIFFICULT

NO.	HIKE NAME	RATING	BEST MONTHS	KIDS	DOGS
14.	Towell Falls	★	Apr–May, Oct–Nov	✔	✔
16.	Bowl and Pitcher Loop	★★★	Apr–Jun, Sep–Oct	✔	✔
19.	Knothead Loop	★★★★	Apr–Nov	✔	✔
24.	Dishman Hills Loop	★★★	Mar–Oct	✔	✔
27.	Saltese Conservation Area	★★	May–Sep	✔	✔
28.	Antoine Peak	★★★	May–Oct	✔	✔
31.	Day Mountain–Mount Kit Carson Traverse	★★★★	Jun–Sep		✔

NO.	HIKE NAME	RATING	BEST MONTHS	KIDS	DOGS
33.	Vista House	★★★★★	Jun-Sep	✔	✔
34.	Quartz Mountain Lookout	★★★★	Jun-Oct	✔	✔
36.	Bead Lake	★★★★	May-Sep	✔	✔
37.	Kamiak Butte	★★★	Apr-Sep	✔	✔
41.	Mineral Ridge	★★	May-Sep, Dec	✔	✔
44.	Indian Cliffs and CCC Loops	★★★★	Apr-Oct	✔	✔
48.	Trail of the Coeur d'Alenes, Harrison–Gray's Meadow	★★★	Apr-Oct	✔	✔
59.	Pulaski Trail	★★★★	May-Sep	✔	✔
60.	Marie Creek	★★★	May-Oct	✔	✔
69.	Trestle Peak	★★★	Jun-Sep	✔	✔
70.	Lake Darling	★★★★	Jul-Sep	✔	✔
71.	Lake Estelle	★★★★★	Jun-Sep		✔
73.	Harrison Lake	★★★★★	Jun-Sep	✔	✔

DIFFICULT

NO.	HIKE NAME	RATING	BEST MONTHS	KIDS	DOGS
20.	Little Spokane Upstream	★★★	Apr-Jun, Sep-Oct		✔
23.	Pine Bluff Loop	★★★★	Apr-Jun, Sep-Oct		✔
25.	Big Rock Loop	★★★★	Apr-Oct	✔	✔
29.	Liberty Creek Loop	★★★★	May-Sep		✔
32.	Beauty Mountain Loop	★★★★	Jun-Oct		✔
42.	Mount Coeur d'Alene	★★★	May-Oct		✔
45.	Whitetail Loop	★★	Apr-Sep		✔
63.	North Chilco Peak	★★★★	Jun-Sep		✔
65.	Gold Hill Trail	★★★	May-Sep		✔
68.	Mickinnick Trail	★★★★	May-Oct		✔
72.	Moose Mountain Loop	★★★★★	Jun-Sep		✔
74.	The Green Monarch	★	May-Sep		✔

EXTREME

NO.	HIKE NAME	RATING	BEST MONTHS	KIDS	DOGS
58.	Coal Creek	★★	Jun-Sep		✔
75.	Scotchman Peak	★★★★★	Jun-Sep		✔

ACKNOWLEDGMENTS

It was my wife, B. B. Hardbody, who talked me into writing this book. She convinced and cajoled me and finally got me believing I could get off the couch and away from my desk, then get into good enough shape to waddle along on the hikes described here. I was pretty much certain I'd wimp out somewhere along the way, but her continuing encouragement kept me going. I'd fake a limp or begin faux-panting, and she'd coax me along with a few kind words, like, "Get moving or I'll leave you to the vultures."

I am also extremely grateful to Gary Luke and all of the good people at Sasquatch Books who had faith that I could complete this project given the fact that I am older than the Missoula Floods. And I want to thank David Nelson, editor of the *Kitsap Sun*, who still finds space in his newspaper for my weekly outdoors column, as well as all three of my readers for their support.

As always, I'm most appreciative of the hundreds of volunteers who keep our trails in such good condition. Thanks go to the employees of the US Forest Service and National Park Service as well, for their work in keeping our wilderness pathways open.

INTRODUCTION

Seventy-five hikes. Seventy-five days. Seventy-five years old.

I would like to tell you that we—B. B. Hardbody and I—trekked all of those more than five hundred miles on consecutive days. And we might have, had I not been crippled early on by an overuse injury to my left ankle. Bad things like that happen to people who spend six months sitting on their butts trying to write entertaining and informative guides to our best Northwest trails. Then, like hibernating bears, they waddle forth in the spring and imagine they can hike eight or nine miles in three hours without suffering consequences.

Maybe they could waddle three miles an hour for three hours once upon a time, a quarter of a century ago. But not in 2016, when my wife and I traversed all of the pathways outlined on the following pages. We began in mid-April and arrived at the summit of Scotchman Peak (Hike 75) in early September. During that period, we gained a new perspective on nature's beauty, met some interesting and friendly people, and learned valuable lessons about walking in an environment vastly different from anywhere either of us had hiked in at least five decades.

For me, it was a nostalgic half year. I revisited some of the trails I walked more than sixty years ago as one of George Libby's "Iron Men"—a title he bestowed upon the boys who were foolish enough to follow him into the wooded hills south of Dishman or north of Hutton Settlement on cold, rainy autumn Saturdays. Libby, a portrait photographer, led weekly hikes around the Spokane area for more than forty years, ran summer camps at Liberty and Coeur d'Alene Lakes, and directed National Rifle Association marksmanship classes at the old Spokane Armory for much of that time. He died in 1973 at the age of ninety-three, leaving generations of Spokane youth with a greater appreciation and knowledge of the great outdoors.

I've spent most of my adult life day hiking, backpacking, and skiing in Washington's Cascade and Olympic Mountains, with vacation backpacks and treks around Northwest national parks and forests in Alaska, Montana, Oregon, British Columbia, and Alberta.

I mostly cut my day-hiking chops in Olympic National Park and Forest, largely because for the first couple decades of my working life, I was unable to wrangle two consecutive days off. I'd drive to trailheads at night, camp, and trek as far as my legs would take me in a day. Many times, that turned out to be twenty miles or more. It was a blessing in disguise because on most weekday hikes, I had the wilderness all to myself and my hiking partner. Meeting another wildland pedestrian was a rarity, even at a time when hiking and backpacking were "trending." The same lack of pedestrian company was true in the Olympic and Mount Rainier National Park winters, when I took up backcountry skiing in the early 1970s.

Though B. B. Hardbody was raised in Spokane and Montana, and learned about the Inland Northwest outdoors through a love of falconry, she gained most of her backcountry experience by hiking and climbing in Alaska, where she summited Denali, raised a son alone, and put herself through college.

So walking the trails around our native Spokane was a reawakening to the extreme differences in Northwest hiking from west of the Cascade Mountains to east of them, from what's underfoot to what falls (or doesn't) from the sky. Thanks to the Cascades, hiking in this neck of the woods is a harsh contrast to walking trails anywhere else in the state.

Not that there isn't variety. You'll find arguably greater differences in Inland Northwest hiking trails than any west of the Cascades. Around here, you can walk trails where "woods" don't even exist, or find fern-festooned forests nearly as thick as you'd wade in an Olympic rain forest. Clay or sand footpaths around here are tamped so hard in places it feels like you're walking on asphalt; mud wallows as rare as pig bristles on a goose. One of the obvious contrasts is the abundance here of blue sky above your head: seventy-three of our seventy-five hiking days were sunny. Ironically, the single day it rained steadily upon us was along a lake shoreline where a cooling swim would have been welcome on any of the forty hot days that followed.

The relative absence of precipitation during the hiking season—Spokane averages around 19 inches every year—is both a boon and bane for hikers. Wildlife watchers will appreciate the fact that they can see at least three times farther into Inland Northwest pine forests than they can anywhere west of the Cascade crest. Navigation on- and off-trail is far easier here than it is forging your path through the vine maple and alder on the wet side of the mountains. But that same lack of lush forest–producing rain means fewer opportunities to refill your water bottle or find cooling shade. And in some cases, it seems you must haul half your weight in H_2O while you drag yourself, panting and wheezing, along the Columbia Plateau State Park Trail on a 95-degree July day, wondering why in the hell you are still carrying that damned umbrella in your pack, except maybe it would work to give you some shade and why didn't you think of that before putting the pack on because it's too much work to take it off and fish around the what-now-has-to-be-melted Reese's and hey, some of that fine New Boundary Brewery Renegade Red sounds pretty excellent right now . . .

Or maybe that's just me.

This region's many pathways owe their existence to the industries that in large part created Spokane, Coeur d'Alene, and Sandpoint: railroads, forests, mining, and farming. They, in turn, can trace many of their wild routes to the Native Americans who walked them for centuries before later arrivals. Perhaps that helps to explain the striking differences in the level, easy trails that follow old rail corridors and the steep, purposeful pathways of timber cruisers and prospectors leading to mountain forests. While total elevation gained on a Cascade or Olympic hike is almost certainly greater than any in this region, be assured that when it's time to climb around here, you'll find short pitches generally steeper than elsewhere in the state.

Another marked contrast between hikes here and across our sunset mountains is the relative proximity to civilization that we enjoy. Trailheads providing everything from sage-decorated basalt steppes to cedar-draped creeks can be found less than thirty minutes from Spokane, Sandpoint, or Coeur d'Alene. In some cases, they're within walking distance from downtown. Thus you'll find pedestrians plying pathways during their lunch hour or jogging along the South Hill bluff before heading to work. They hike trails that might not feel as wild and woolly as an Olympic or North Cascades National Park venue, but both yield a chance to enjoy the out-of-doors.

Probably because Washington's three national parks prohibit biking on most of the trails and national forests west of the Cascades, we were initially surprised to see many more cyclists and equestrians on Inland Northwest pathways. We counted more two-wheeled and four-hoofed hikers than two-legged ones on several hikes. We were thankful that despite our relative lack of experience in sharing the trail, every mountain biker we encountered was accustomed to meeting pedestrians. They were courteous and always warned us when approaching from behind. One guy who passed us clanged like Big Ben, a cowbell dangling and jangling from his handlebars.

To sum up: carry water and ditch the umbrella, watch for mountain bikes and equestrians (and they'll watch for you). Most of all, I hope you enjoy the following hikes.

—Seabury Blair Jr.

USING THIS GUIDE

The beginning of each trail description is intended to give you quick information that can help you decide whether the specific day hike is one that interests you. Here's what you'll find:

Trail Number & Name

Trails are numbered in this guide following a geographical order; see the Overview Map on page vii for general location. Trail names usually reflect those names used by the National Forest Service and other land managers. In some cases, portions of very long trails or multiple sections of separate trails have been combined into a single hike and assigned a new name.

Overall Rating

Assigning an overall rating to a hike is a difficult task, given the fact that one hiker's preferred trail is another's dung heap. Yet every trail in this guide is worth walking (we're still working on the dung-heap trail guide). Here, the difference between a five-star hike and one with four stars might only be the number and variety of wildflowers along the trail, or the height of the tripping tree roots arrayed on the path before you. The trails in this book are the best you'll find in the Inland Northwest, but you are invited to try all of the ones we've excluded. (See Resources on page 269.)

Another problem is attempting to be objective in rating the trails. Some of us are pushovers for trails above timberline, where the wildflowers wave in gentle summer breezes, where mountains claw clouds, and where cooling snowfields linger through late spring. Hikes with these features may be rated higher than you might rate them, especially if you love walking along rattling rivers or padding on pine forest paths softened by last autumn's needles. Rating one hike higher than another might come down to something as simple as stepping in a pile of horse manure while watching a hawk soar, or running out of water in summer with a mile farther to the Palouse trailhead.

Finally, many factors must be considered in assigning an overall rating. Besides all that aesthetic stuff like scenery and wildlife, there are objective criteria like trail condition, length and steepness, and obstacles like creek crossings or deadfalls. In the end, all that really matters is that you enjoy the hike—not whether you agree with our rating. That said, our rating follows.

★ This hike is worth taking, even with your in-laws.

★★ Expect to discover socially and culturally redeeming values on this hike. Or, at least, very fine scenery.

★★★ You would be willing to get up before sunrise to take this hike, even if you watched a Star Wars marathon the night before.

★★★★ This is the Häagen-Dazs of hikes; if you don't like ice cream, a hike with this rating will give more pleasure than any favorite comfort food.

★★★★★ The aesthetic and physical rewards are so great that hikes given this rating are considered sinful by many conservative religions.

Distance

The distance listed is round-trip, exclusive of any side trips to view-points or other features mentioned along the way. If these excursions off the main trail are longer than 0.2 mile, that distance will be mentioned in the description of the hike.

Note: In an effort to prove that trails are indeed getting longer as I grow older, I once pushed a bike wheel equipped with a cyclometer around most of the trails in an earlier guidebook. I learned to my disappointment that most trails aren't getting longer, although there are notable exceptions.

For this guide, I relied on Fitbits both B. B. Hardbody and I carried, as well as a Garmin Forerunner and GPS-enabled iPad supplemented with a Dual GPS receiver and the excellent app iHikeGPS, which not only gave me trail distances—rounded to the nearest tenth of a mile—and profiles, but traced my routes on USGS topographic maps. You can probably guess that on many of our hikes, none of these devices agreed with one another on how far we had walked. In such cases, we added the disparate digits and averaged them.

Hiking Time

This is an estimate of the time it takes the average hiker to walk the trail, round-trip. Since none of us are average hikers, you may feel free to ignore this entry. For the most part, however, the pace on the trail is calculated at 2 miles per hour. Times are estimated conservatively; even so, this rate might slow on trails with significant elevation gain. Some hikers will wonder what sort of trail slug came up with such ridiculously long hiking times, and this trail slug is okay with that.

Elevation Gain

This is a calculation of the total number of feet you'll have to climb on the trail. Don't assume that all of the elevation will be gained on the way to your destination. Some of these trails actually lose elevation on the way and gain it on the return, or alternately gain and lose elevation along the way. The certainty is that on a round-trip hike, you always gain the same amount of elevation that you lose.

High Point

This is the highest point above sea level you'll reach on any given hike.

Difficulty

Here's another tough one. Experienced hikers might find a hike rated "Moderately Difficult" to be only "Moderate," while beginning trekkers might rate the same walk "Difficult." As with hiking times, the difficulty level of individual hikes was rated conservatively. Incidentally, it is far easier to rate a hike conservatively now that I am three-quarters of a century toward pushing up cheatgrass.

The terms used to describe difficulty are as follows:

- ◆ Easy: Few, if any hills; generally between 1 and 4 miles round-trip; suitable for families with small children.

- ◆◆ Moderate: Longer, gently graded hills; generally 4 to 6 miles round-trip.

- ◆◆◆ Moderately Difficult: Steeper grades; elevation changes greater than about 1,000 feet; between 6 and 9 miles round-trip.

- ◆◆◆◆ Difficult: Sustained, steep climbs of at least 1 mile; elevation gain and loss greater than 1,500 feet; usually more than 7 miles round-trip. Your deodorant may fail you on these hikes.

- ◆◆◆◆◆ Extreme: Sustained steep climbs; distances greater than 8 miles round-trip. These trails will provide a rigorous test of your hiking skills and muscles.

Best Months

Here you'll find our recommendation for the best months of the year to take any given hike. Trails that are open throughout the year or that make good three-season hikes will be indicated here.

Permits/Contact

This entry will tell you whether you need a Discover Pass or must pay any permit or fee on any hike, along with the land manager to contact for more information.

Maps

I've taken to recommending United States Geological Survey (USGS) quadrangle maps for all hikes, which can now be found on a number of apps offering seamless coordination between quadrangles. Although you'll find excellent US Forest Service maps for some of the hikes in this guide, as well as good maps produced by local land managers, USGS quads are now the standard by which I measure all maps, including any available from internet sources.

Ⓟ	Parking Area
——	Road
——	Trail Route
·········	Alternate Route
⟶	Direction of Travel
↰	Turnaround Point
=	Bridge
5880'	Elevation
III	Falls
90	Interstate Highway
99	US Highway
97	State Highway
9	Forest Highway

Contour Interval 40 Feet/Scale Varies

Each hike in this book includes a trail map of the route, featuring parking and trailhead, alternate routes, direction, elevation profile, and more. B. B. Hardbody's maps are based on USGS maps, with our steps traced by the aforementioned iPad, iHikeGPS, and Dual GPS receiver. If you look closely, you might see a few cases where either the trail has altered from the original on the USGS quad, or (less likely) the mapmaker missed the actual route. Use the legend above.

Trail Notes

Look here for a quick guide to trail regulations and features like leashed dogs OK, pets prohibited, and bikes welcome.

After the at-a-glance overview of each hike, you'll find detailed descriptions in the short sections that follow:

The Hike

This is an attempt to convey the feel of the trail in a sentence or two, including the type of trail and whether there's a one-way hiking option.

Getting There

You'll either find out how to get to the trailhead or, God forbid, I'll get you hopelessly lost. New to this section is information on bus routes that take you to or very near the trailhead. The elevation at the trailhead is included at the end of this section.

I've tried to group the hikes along major highway corridors. In this guide, those would include Interstate 90 and US Routes 5, 195, and 395, as well as several Washington and Idaho State Routes.

The Trail

Here's where you'll get the blow-by-blow, mile-by-mile description of the trail. It's information your feet will find useful, and we apologize if, every now and then, we take time to recognize a Magnificent Mountain or Awesome Ponderosa, since you're admirably equipped to recognize those features yourself. We'll advise you here as well of any unique historic or cultural notes that aren't so obvious.

Going Farther

You can learn good options for a longer walk in this section, which is certain to be helpful to all you young whippersnappers out there. Possible side trips from the same trailhead will be pointed out, and we'll mention nearby public campgrounds that might get you on the trail sooner.

Other Hikes

The end of some chapters will include a sentence or two describing other trails in the area that you might want to explore, or hikes that fall outside out a 90-minute drive from Spokane, Sandpoint, or Coeur d'Alene.

BE CAREFUL

It is all too easy on a warm, sunny day on the trail to forget all of the stuff you ought to be carrying in your pack. Day hikers, especially, are likely to leave that extra layer or rain parka in the trunk. Some folks even forget that most essential item—a hiking partner. Ignore this rule and you might wind up cutting off your own arm.

Virtually every time, day hikers who forget one or two of the basic rules for safe wilderness travel return to the trailhead smiling and healthy. No trail cop is going to cite you for negligent hiking if you have only nine of the so-called "Ten Essentials," or if you hit the trail without registering or telling someone where you're going.

The Ten Essential "Systems"

Those clever Mountaineers, a Seattle-based club with chapters throughout the state (including a lively Spokane chapter), are always certain to stay abreast of trends. Today we live in a world of "systems"—as in "life support system" or "total system failure"—so the Mountaineers, which came up with the original Ten Essentials, modified the list some years back to the Ten Essential Systems in the excellent manual *Mountaineering: The Freedom of the Hills.* You'll have no difficulty figuring out what those systems are from the classic list: map, compass, sunglasses and sunscreen, extra clothing, headlamp/flashlight, first aid supplies, firestarter, matches, knife, and extra food.

Here's the official, unabridged, and wholly redundant list of the essential systems:

- A **navigation system**, which unsurprisingly consists of a map and compass. It might also include a Global Positioning System or any of a number of GPS-enabled apps—but if you rely on electronic devices to determine where to go, always carry a spare energy system (battery) along. Remember too that a GPS can tell you where you are and how to get home, but it can't tell you if you're about to step off a cliff while looking down at your phone.

- A **sun protection system**, which as you might guess consists of sunglasses and sunscreen. Even the Mountaineers couldn't find anything to add to this one—but if you carry a lightweight umbrella system for shade on the Columbia Plateau State Park Trail, nobody will call you out.

- An **insulation system**, or extra clothing. That might be long underwear, insulating top and bottom layers, rain- or windproof layers, or a hat/cap and gloves or mittens. Or you might prefer an insulation system that includes a body-sized box of rigid foam insulation, light enough to tote on day hikes and serving as an emergency shelter system as well.

- An **illumination system**, or if you wish, a headlamp or flashlight with extra bulb and batteries. Alternative illumination systems might include a carbide miner's lamp or emergency flares—which could double as your fire system or reduce the weight of your insulation system. Headlamps and flashlights with light-emitting diodes (LEDs) and lithium batteries burn longer than other illumination systems but may deplete your financial accounting system.

- A **first aid supplies system**. It should come as no surprise that this system includes a first aid kit and little else. You may feel free to try to drag your family physician along instead, though I suppose a nurse would do just as well, except in emergencies involving surgical procedures. A minimal first aid system for day hikers should include wraps for sprains or an ankle support system, plus a blister treatment system.

- A **fire system**, better known as waterproof matches and a firestarter.

- A **repair kit and tools system**, described in the classic list as a pocketknife. Thanks to the Swiss Army and folks like Leatherman, a day hiker needn't have much of a repair kit and tools system. One of either could open almost any beer or wine container, as well as fell a small pine.

- A **nutrition system**. Unless you are into packing an IV unit, make it extra food.

- A **hydration system**—also known as water.

- An **emergency shelter system**, which should be no problem if you opt for a rigid foam insulation system. One of those lightweight plastic/foil blankets or bags might work better.

In addition to those systems, most day hikers never hit the trail without toting a toilet paper system in a plastic bag and perhaps some type of bug repellent system on summer hikes. A loud emergency whistle system is a lightweight addition. A visual-aid system (binoculars) is worth its weight simply for watching wildlife systems and might help you find your route if you lose the trail system.

Consider a walking stick or trekking pole system, which can take the stress off your joint system on steep trails, or help steady you while crossing stream systems. In emergencies, they can serve as shelter support systems or hold feral Pomeranians at bay.

Now, if anytime in describing the hikes that follow I use the word "system," you may feel free to choke, stab, freeze, or burn me with any of the Ten Essentials.

Water

Dehydration is one of the most common ailments that day hikers face, especially in the arid Inland Northwest. No one should head out on the trail without at least one liter of drinking water per person. Around this neck of the woods, two liters is better.

While there are limited opportunities to refill your water bottle on some of the hikes outlined in this book, don't rely on streams, which are often difficult to reach and dry in late summer. It is better to assume water is not available on any hike. In cases where it is, this will be mentioned in the trail description.

Treat all water in the wilderness as if it were contaminated. The most worrisome problem might be a little critter called *Giardia lamblia*, which can give you a case of the trots that you'll never forget. The most noticeable symptom of giardiasis is "explosive diarrhea." Eeeewwww.

We can all be thankful there is an easy way to ensure that the water you take from a stream or lake is safe to drink. When used properly, filter pumps eliminate at least 99.9 percent of giardia and other dangerous organisms from the water. A recent and far more convenient addition to filter pumps, especially for day hikers, is the relatively inexpensive water bottle equipped with its own filter. You simply fill the bottle from the stream or lake (taking extreme care not to contaminate the mouthpiece or drinking cap), drop the filter into place, screw on the top, and you're ready to drink filtered water. Another lightweight alternative to the filter bottle is a straw that delivers potable water and eliminates the bottle altogether.

Many veteran hikers still choose to forego all this gadgetry and use the old-fashioned method: iodine water treatments, which come in tablets or crystals. The taste might be objectionable to some, but it's a guaranteed way to kill giardia and any other waterborne bugs—something a filter, especially an improperly used or maintained one, is not.

Another quick and easy treatment for wild water is to use a device that employs UV light to purify the H_2O. It's portable and lightweight, and can be used multiple times. The downside: it operates on batteries, so make certain you're charged and always carry spares. Another issue is that even though everything in the water that can hurt you has been killed, water taken from a muddy source still looks like something you wouldn't let your in-laws drink.

Weather

The Selkirk Mountains generate typical alpine weather, which can change rapidly and with little warning. On most any mountain hike during the fall or spring, you should be prepared to be snowed, rained, or sleeted upon; be blown around; and probably get sunburned—all in the span of a day. Hikers in Washington's mountains have frozen to death in July and drowned in the afternoon while fording flood-filled rivers that were shallow in the morning. Mother Nature is most often a friendly, generous old lady who bakes cookies and bread for you, but when you least expect it, she dons a goalie's mask and whacks at you with an icicle or lightning bolt. So be prepared, scouts.

Possibly the greatest weather-related hazard an Inland Northwest hiker will face is heat. Summer temperatures average 85 degrees Fahrenheit throughout the region and the season: average high temperatures in Sandpoint, Coeur d'Alene, and Spokane are the same in July as they are in August and barely drop a few degrees in June. Days pushing the mercury above 100 degrees Fahrenheit are not uncommon. Take most of your hikes in the Palouse or sage country west of Cheney in the early morning or evening; or better yet, save these hikes for the spring, fall, or even winter. Enjoy hikes in the mountains or along lakes, rivers, or streams during the summer, where a chance to cool off is a possibility.

Learn to recognize and treat the symptoms of heat exhaustion and heatstroke. Carry enough water to have some left for a final drink back at the trailhead. Take rest stops in the shade wherever possible. Wear wide-brimmed hats and lightweight clothing that wicks moisture and protects you from UV rays. The Inland Northwest is one region where the admonition about wearing cotton can be ignored altogether—assuming you've stashed a windproof and rain-resistant layer in your pack.

Wind is another weather factor to deal with in this neck of the woods. Though rarely strong enough to topple trees or cause you to call off a hike, it can be pesky when it stirs up dust devils along the Columbia Plateau State Park Trail or whips your cap off while you're trying to pick your way through the Chilco Mountain talus.

A hazard more common to the Inland Northwest is lightning. Thunderstorms often blow in during afternoon hikes and can sometimes be avoided altogether by keeping an eye out for those huge, billowing, dark cumulonimbus clouds or watching for distant lightning strikes. While being struck by lightning is extremely rare, learn common avoidance techniques like staying away from water, metallic objects, and open spaces; not walking in groups; and seeking low ground. The best advice on never catching a bolt that I've found comes from Richard Kithil Jr., CEO of the National Lightning Safety Institute: "Treat lightning like a snake: if you see it or hear it, take evasive measures."

Flora and Fauna

Speaking of snakes, the Inland Northwest has all the snakes Saint Patrick drove out of Ireland, plus a few more. You can spot the Irish snakes because they are fond of swimming in salt water and carry shillelaghs. (Feel free to check my research on this.) My advice: treat all snakes like lightning; if you see one or hear one, take evasive measures.

Rattlesnakes are found in this region, especially in the dry, rocky lands to the west of Spokane. They are also the most easily avoided critters you'll find around here. Stay on the trail, keep your eyes on the path in front of you, and listen for the telltale buzz of a rattlesnake alarm. We didn't encounter a single slippery snake in the thirty or more hikes we took in prime rattler country during the summer.

Another animal capable of doing you serious harm is the grizzly bear, which is also very easy to avoid. Since all North American bears—black or griz—are capable of hurting you, there's not much point in identifying which is which. Treat any bear you see as if it's a grizzly and you'll have no problem. Keep your distance; make noise while hiking in bear country and especially in forests or brush where visibility is restricted. Travel in groups.

The rare bear sightings to the south and west of Spokane are most likely black bears. Black bears are also more likely to be encountered closer to suburban areas or sometimes even in suburban areas. Black bears are generally more eager to avoid you than vice versa and will probably run off if you find them lumbering along the trail. You're more likely to see a grizzly bear in the spring and fall in the high country to the north and east of Spokane. Only ten or fifteen of the hikes in this guide trespass on common grizzly territory, and you'll find mention of that fact in the text. Still, encounters with this occasionally threatening animal occur every year, so a cautious hiker is advised to carry bear spray such as Counter Assault on these hikes. Practice drawing and arming the canister, perhaps even discharging a short burst to see how it disperses and how the recoil causes you to shoot high. You can find complete instructions for how to use bear spray online.

Another animal once considered benign is the mountain goat, which might be encountered on several of the hikes described in this guide. They've become such pests around Scotchman Peak (Hike 75) that Friends of Scotchman Peaks Wilderness has posted educational signs along the trail and weekend volunteers inform hikers about these splendid alpine climbers. But mountain goats are much more than pests. They can be killers, as Olympic National Park hiker Robert Boardman tragically discovered in 2010. An aggressive billy gored him in the leg then stood over him to keep his hiking partners away while Boardman bled to death on the trail. Other hikers reported incidents of charging and injuries by goats in the Olympic Mountains.

Mountain goats in the Inland Northwest so far have only been treated as nuisances that chew on pack straps or other items that might be salty from sweat. Try to keep at least fifty yards away from goats at all times. Calmly retreat down the trail if the goat exhibits threatening behavior, such as bowing its head and pointing its horns at you. If you've done all you can to keep your distance and it continues to move toward you, try to scare it off by shouting, blowing a whistle, or throwing rocks. Though I have asked officials repeatedly, I have never had a definitive answer about the effectiveness of bear spray on mountain goats.

Moose might also be viewed on many of the hikes described in this book, including rare sightings within the city limits of Spokane, Sandpoint, or Coeur d'Alene. They're most often seen during spring and fall, seasons when they might also be the most aggressive. More often than not, a moose sighting is likely to be just that, and you can consider yourself lucky to watch the largest member of the deer family. The average moose weighs more than 1,200 pounds, which means that if it decides it doesn't want you around, you have the equivalent of a 1960 Volkswagen Beetle charging you. So keep your distance, don't approach the animal, and above all, don't piss it off.

Two animals found in the Inland Northwest are likely never seen by day hikers: wolves and cougars. Wolves are relocating throughout Eastern Washington, particularly in the northeast, and have been seen as little as fifteen miles north of Spokane. Because they are so stealthy and reclusive, cougars are seldom encountered, but you might hear them scream at night or see their tracks on just about any trail in the Selkirks. In the extremely unlikely event one of these predators decides to treat you as a potential meal, follow the advice from the Washington Department of Fish and Wildlife:

Cougar: Don't take your eyes off the cougar. Make yourself appear big by raising your arms above your head, open your jacket if you're wearing one, and wave your hiking poles above your head. If the cougar approaches, yell and throw rocks, sticks, anything your can get your hands on. In the event of an attack, fight back aggressively.

Wolf: Try to make yourself look larger, make noise, and throw rocks or sticks while slowly backing away. Try to stare the wolf down and don't turn your back on the wolf. Keep your dog on a leash.

Now that you're sufficiently worried about the least likely encounters with potentially dangerous wildlife, I'll tell you about the one you'll almost certainly face: the wood tick. They are so common in the Inland Northwest during spring and summer that most elementary school children know how to remove the little suckers. These micro-vampires can carry disease, including Rocky Mountain spotted fever. They wait on grasses and shrubs for warm-blooded animals—I'm guessing that includes most of you—to walk by. Cousins to the spider, they climb aboard as you pass and can spend up to twenty-four hours exploring your body, looking for the best place to dig in and start sucking your blood. More often than not, they find those places to be your hairline or crotch. Again, eeeewwww.

You can easily spot ticks on your body as they search for a meal. They are about the size of this *o*, and sometimes tickle you as they stroll around. So examine yourself after every hike and make certain to check your dog as well. If you find one that has already dug in, grasp the head with tweezers as close as possible to your skin and pull gently and steadily to remove it. Wash the area with a disinfectant and examine the bite mark regularly for signs of a rash, which would indicate a visit to the doctor.

As with any of the wildlife mentioned here, ticks and their bites can easily be avoided. Wear long-sleeved shirts and long pants tucked into socks. Spray permethrin on pant legs and shirtsleeves to repel ticks—

DEET is more effective but eats certain fabrics and might be harmful for children. We ran into a hiker along the Little Spokane River who tucked his trousers into long gaiters and told us it was most effective at keeping ticks at bay.

Other common hazards to day hikers include stinging and biting pests like yellow jackets (particularly in late summer and early autumn), black flies, mosquitoes, and deer flies. Liberal doses of insect repellent can take care of the mosquitoes and flies but may not keep those pesky yellow jackets away.

Poison oak and ivy are both found in profusion in the Inland Northwest, particularly in lowland forests and meadows. Stinging nettles can be found along streams and in wet areas but don't represent the kind of long misery you'll endure after a close encounter with the poison ivy kind. These shiny, three-leaved mini-monsters can whack your exposed skin with rash and even blisters that can last for weeks. The oil on poison oak and ivy can get on clothing and pets as well as your skin and is difficult to wash off. Learn to recognize poison ivy, oak, and nettles, and avoid contact with them all. In the event of contamination, the best treatment is to apply any of several products made to neutralize the oil from the plant. These might include any of the Tecnu products or IvyX. A national forest field worker once told me that mechanic's hand cleaner worked just as well, but I didn't have the guts to test it.

Finally, don't let any of the preceding discourage you from getting out on any of the trails that follow. We've been hiking the better part of five decades, and neither B. B. Hardbody nor I have yet to get lost (although I have been terribly confused about which direction to go several times—B. B. always straightens me out), be menaced by wild animals, be attacked by killer bees, or be swept away in a flash flood. So tighten your bootlaces, shoulder that pack, and get out on one of the hikes that follow. We'll see you on the trail!

Trail Etiquette and Hiking Ethics

On any of the shorter hikes close to urban or suburban areas in this guide, you're likely to run into (not literally, I hope) some folks who don't walk trails much or aren't schooled in trekking manners. I have resisted the urge to bodycheck runners blasting down a trail while I am waddling up it, and I've seen hikers who haven't the foggiest notion of what to do upon encountering an equestrian. Simply put, the general rules of etiquette are:

- Hikers and bicyclists yield to horses.
- Downhill hikers yield to uphill hikers unless the uphill hiker steps aside, inviting the downhill pedestrian to pass. I have discovered this is an excellent maneuver to slow my heartbeat to a nonlethal rate.
- Bicyclists should yield to hikers, but because mountain bicyclists are moving faster than hikers, it might be more prudent for pedestrians to get out of the way of two-wheelers. It just makes good sense.

Finally, to protect the splendid Inland Northwest landscape so future generations can enjoy it just as much as you do, take the following suggestions to heart. Stay on established trails, don't cut switchbacks, and stay off sensitive areas. Leave no trace, pack out your trash, and respect other trail users. And because you're having such a great time hiking the trails described next, why not volunteer your service by lending a hand on a trail building or repair project? Check the list of outdoors organizations on page 269.

URBAN SPOKANE

---

1. Downtown River Walk

RATING	DISTANCE	HIKING TIME
★★★☆☆	5.3 miles round-trip	2.5 hours

ELEVATION GAIN	HIGH POINT	DIFFICULTY
200 feet	1,960 feet	◆◆◆◆◆

BEST MONTHS
Jan Feb **Mar Apr May Jun Jul Aug Sep Oct** Nov Dec

The Hike

Here's an urban stroll that is an excellent muscle-powered way to see the best and newest sections of the city's downtown showcase park and trail.

Getting There

Take exit 280 from Interstate 90 and turn left on Walnut Street. Follow Walnut underneath I-90 and turn right on 3rd Avenue. Drive one block to Cedar Street and turn left. Drive three blocks north, keeping to the right at 1st Avenue. Turn left onto Sprague Avenue and West Riverside Avenue. Follow West Riverside through historic Browne's Addition downhill to Clarke Avenue, and turn right into a large parking area at the People's Park section of High Bridge Park. The trailhead is at 1,760 feet above sea level. Restrooms are available.

A Spokane Transit Authority bus route runs past the trailhead on Clarke Avenue. Call (509) 328-RIDE or visit SpokaneTransit.com.

PERMITS/CONTACT
None required/Spokane City Parks and Recreation,
(509) 625-6200, www.spokaneparks.org

MAPS
USGS Spokane SW; city map

TRAIL NOTES
Leashed dogs OK; bikes welcome

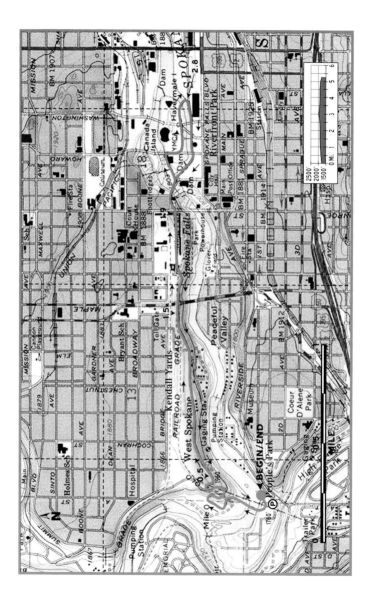

Spokane skyline from the Centennial Trail near Kendall Yards

The Trail

This walk takes you up the flower-decked bluff of the Herbert M. Hamblen Conservation Area to Kendall Yards, a new residential area reclaimed from an old rail facility where you can find shops and cafés overlooking the Spokane River. You'll look across at the city from the 39-mile-long Centennial Trail, cross the tumbling Spokane River into Riverfront Park, and revisit childhood on the antique Looff Carrousel. Though the trail is accessible year-round, the best time might be the early spring, when bluffs are abloom with arrowleaf balsamroot and the Spokane River falls are in full roar.

The People's Park area of Spokane's High Bridge Park has a colorful reputation that includes public nudity and other activities we civilized patricians simply cannot abide. Regardless, head toward that spiffy Sandifur Memorial Bridge and cross the Spokane River before beginning the single major climb of this hike, 200 vertical feet up a paved pathway to Kendall Yards. The entire trail is paved, and this is probably the only section where most wheelchair hikers might need assistance. You'll find benches along the way if you wish to rest.

At the top of the hillside, **0.5** mile from the trailhead, find a viewpoint overlooking the river and across to the city skyline. To the left are the new townhouse condominiums of Kendall Yards and the shops and restaurants that make the area one of Spokane's newest and best places for city living. The Centennial Trail passes in front of the buildings, and you can cruise along the level path for 2.1 miles, ducking under Maple Street Bridge at **1.5** miles and the Monroe Street Bridge in another 0.4 mile. The section under the Monroe bridge affords an excellent view of falls on the Spokane River.

Just past the bridge, follow Bridge Avenue to the east and take the Lincoln Street Bridge across the river to Riverfront Park. Pedestrian bridges upriver to Canada Island (renamed snxw meneʔ in the Salish language in March 2017) also serve up great fall-watching platforms. Turn left across the Lincoln bridge and follow the paved pathway onto Havermale Island, the site of Expo '74. The park and island are undergoing a major redesign, but you should be able to find a route that heads east along the river to a pedestrian bridge that crosses south to another section of the trail that passes the Spokane Opera House, **2.8** miles from the trailhead.

Turn right and walk west through the park, where you'll likely find the Looff Carrousel, which has given memories to Spokane youngsters—and adults—since 1909. It too was recently scheduled for a face-lift, but you can be certain you'll find it somewhere along your path. After you've seen all that the park has to offer, head back to Lincoln Street and rejoin the trail back to Kendall Yards and the trailhead at **5.3** miles.

Going Farther

You can explore the Centennial Trail to the east from the opera house, crossing and recrossing the Spokane River, for as many miles as you wish. Another option would be circling People's Park and the rest of High Bridge Park, which includes a nice dog park. Just watch out for those naked plebeians. ∎

2. Fish Lake Trail

RATING	DISTANCE	HIKING TIME
★★★ ☆☆	8.0 miles round-trip	5 hours
ELEVATION GAIN	**HIGH POINT**	**DIFFICULTY**
75 feet	1,975 feet	◆◆ ◇◇◇
BEST MONTHS		
~~Jan Feb Mar~~ Apr May Jun Jul Aug Sep Oct ~~Nov Dec~~		

The Hike

Less than 2 miles from downtown hotels, this abandoned rail corridor gives you an excellent way to get out of the city and into pine forest without actually leaving greater Spokane.

Getting There

Take exit 280 from Interstate 90 and follow Walnut Street north to 2nd Avenue. Turn left on 2nd, drive west, and bear left on Sunset Boulevard. Keep to the right of the underpass on Sunset and cross the bridge over Latah Creek. At the first stoplight—Government Way—turn left and drive one block to Milton Street. Turn left and then immediately right into the trailhead parking lot, with its restroom (closed in winter), 1,900 feet above sea level.

Two Spokane Transit Authority bus routes run past the trailhead on Sunset Boulevard. Call (509) 328-RIDE or visit SpokaneTransit.com.

PERMITS/CONTACT
None required/Spokane City Parks and Recreation,
(509) 625-6200, www.spokaneparks.org

MAPS
USGS Spokane SW; city map

TRAIL NOTES
Leashed dogs OK; bikes welcome;
respect private property by staying on the trail

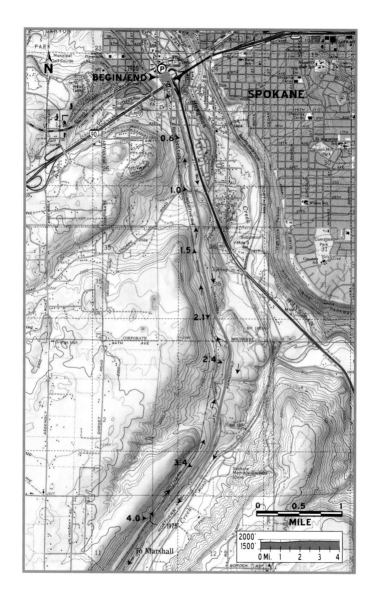

The Trail

The Fish Lake Trail doesn't actually lead to Fish Lake yet, but it is hoped the paved path soon will. It's the first of many great hikes in this guide that owes its existence to railroads. The old Union Pacific Railroad and Spokane city and county got together to give hikers, bicyclists, skaters, and—in winter—cross-country skiers one of the most convenient and comfortable ways to escape the city. After an initial mile or so of listening to traffic noise from I-90 and US Route 195, your woodsy walk turns along a rural road where the only sounds you might hear are reminders that railroads still rule in the Inland Northwest.

Start by walking the paved trail south and crossing a pedestrian bridge over I-90. The pathway is very popular with road bikers and parallels US 195 south for a little over a mile, passing neighboring houses and one of several benches along the route **0.6** mile from the trailhead. At **1.0** mile, marked by a post, cross a bridge passing over Thorpe Road, where you might see wild roses sprouting in the spring, along with lupine and possibly some poison ivy.

Noise decreases as you stray farther from US 195, and at **1.5** miles the only sounds you might hear are songs of meadowlarks in fields and farms to the east and west. You'll turn to the southwest and cross Marshall Road at **2.1** miles, then cross a private driveway at **2.4** miles and soon pass the 3.0-mile marker.

Look across the Cheney-Spokane Road on your left at **3.4** miles to the Spokane Memorial Gardens. Just down the high bank from the trail on the left is Marshall Creek, once a popular juvenile-only fishing spot. The suggested turnaround spot at **4.0** miles overlooks the Marshall Creek valley and pine hills south of the cemetery.

Going Farther

The paved Fish Creek Trail is 9.0 miles one-way. Beyond the suggested turnaround, the route passes above the community of Marshall, once a Northern Pacific rail yard, at 6.8 miles. An alternate trailhead with a restroom is located at Scribner Road, at about 7.1 miles. The trail is blocked at 9.0 miles, above weedy Queen Lucas Lake. ■

3. South Hill Parks Loop

RATING	DISTANCE	HIKING TIME
★ ★ ★ ★ ☆	3.7 miles round-trip	3 hours

ELEVATION GAIN	HIGH POINT	DIFFICULTY
560 feet	2,380 feet	♦ ◇ ◇ ◇ ◇

BEST MONTHS
Jan Feb **Mar Apr May Jun Jul Aug Sep Oct Nov** Dec

The Hike

Tour two of the most beautiful city parks in Spokane and walk along a boulevard of splendid Craftsman homes.

Getting There

Take exit 280 from Interstate 90 and turn right on Maple Street. Follow it to 14th Avenue and turn left. Continue on 14th to Grand Boulevard and turn right. Follow Grand to Manito Park, and turn right on 18th Avenue into the large parking area and beginning of your walk on the right, 2,220 feet above sea level. You'll find a number of restrooms throughout both parks.

A Spokane Transit Authority bus route passes Manito Park on Grand Boulevard, 100 yards from the parking area. Call (509) 328-RIDE or visit SpokaneTransit.com.

PERMITS/CONTACT
None required/Spokane City Parks and Recreation,
(509) 625-6200, www.spokaneparks.org

MAPS
USGS Spokane SW; city map

TRAIL NOTES
Leashed dogs OK (except in Japanese garden); bikes welcome

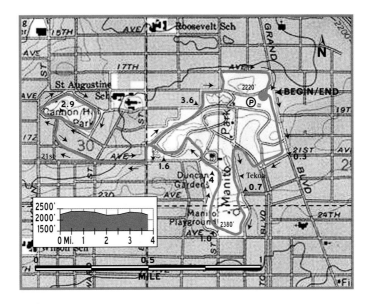

The Trail

More accurately described as sidewalks and urban pathways, this "trail" meanders through two of the oldest and prettiest parks in the city. You'll visit formal and Japanese gardens, a natural pond, a marvelous conservatory, and a popular ice-skating area. It all begins at Manito Park below a grass-covered hill that in winter is covered with hundreds of shrieking, sled-plummeting kids (and not a few shrieking, sled-plummeting adults).

Start by walking east to the sidewalk along Grand Boulevard and turn right, passing a watering trough that was built in 1907 for horse teams climbing the Grand Boulevard hill. Leave the sidewalk here and climb to the top of the sledding hill, then drop through massive old pine trees to Manito Place, **0.3** mile from the trailhead. Turn right and follow Manito Place downhill to Tekoa and turn left along the park. Follow Tekoa to a trail that climbs to the right, just across from 22nd Avenue and **0.7** mile from the trailhead.

The Duncan Gardens make a colorful stop on the Spokane parks tour

This path leads to the Manito playground, where you'll find a sidewalk leading west on 25th Avenue. Walk to Park Drive and a sign noting the park was established in 1904, **1.0** mile from the trailhead. Turn right here and follow Park Drive down to an entrance to the Duncan Gardens, a 3-acre masterpiece of classic European style. Walk north through the gardens past a fountain and climb steps to the Gaiser Conservatory, **1.4** miles from the trailhead. The greenhouse is open year-round and features tropical plants from around the world.

Next, hike west down the hill and cross a road to the entrance of Rose Hill, named by the nonprofit All-America Rose Selections in 2007 as the top rose garden in the nation. More than 150 varieties of roses can be seen here. Cross the garden to the west and follow the road down to the Nishinomiya Tsutakawa Japanese Garden at **1.6** miles. You'll find a koi pond, waterfalls, and a tranquil place for a rest.

Now head west to Bernard Street and turn uphill for a block to 21st Avenue, a sylvan boulevard where a teen motorist—I won't say who—once slid backward down the hill in his father's 1953 Ford in midwinter. Cross Bernard and walk down the hill on 21st, passing splendid old Craftsman homes to Howard Street, one of the few left in the city that is paved with brick that likely came from Cannon Hill Park, a former brickyard and your next stop. Follow 20th Avenue northwest to Post Street, and take Post north a block to Cannon Hill Park.

Walk around the park clockwise, taking in the stonework bridges and buildings. The pond at Cannon Hill was built in the early 1900s where clay was dug for the brickyard two decades earlier. It's a shallow body of water where a young skater—I refuse to name him—once fell through the ice and came close to freezing precious body parts. Once around the park and back to Post Street will net you **2.9** miles from your starting point.

Now climb back up 21st, cross Bernard, and turn past the Japanese garden to the left, walking along the park road and dropping down to Manito Pond where a trail descends to the left at **3.6** miles. A paved walkway circles part of the pond, a natural body of water once named Mirror Lake. Finally, circle the pond, turn left to 17th Avenue, and take a right. Walk two blocks back to Grand and turn right to the parking area.

Going Farther

You can extend your park tour by about 2.5 miles round-trip by turning left on Post Street and walking uphill south to Comstock Park, where you'll find an aquatic center, tennis courts, and ball fields. This is the site where a young boy—who chooses to remain anonymous—once donned a plumed hat and claimed to be one of the Three Musketeers at a school picnic. ∎

4. South Hill Bluff

RATING	DISTANCE	HIKING TIME
★★☆☆☆	4.5 miles round-trip	2 hours
ELEVATION GAIN	HIGH POINT	DIFFICULTY
330 feet	2,140 feet	◆◆◇◇◇

BEST MONTHS											
Jan	Feb	Mar	Apr	May	Jun	Jul	Aug	Sep	Oct	Nov	Dec

The Hike

Here's an urban walk that attracts bicyclists, joggers, and hikers on their lunch break and is within walking distance of downtown Spokane.

Getting There

Take exit 280 from Interstate 90 and turn right on Maple Street, following it uphill to 14th Avenue. Turn right on 14th and drive downhill to the end of the road at Polly Judd Park, the trailhead and restroom, 1,970 feet above sea level.

A Spokane Transit Authority bus route passes 14th on Maple Street, 4 blocks from the trailhead. Call (509) 328-RIDE or visit SpokaneTransit.com.

The Trail

You're never too far from Spokane's rich railroading history on this hike along the steep hillside that plunges up to 600 feet from residential South Hill to the Burlington Northern Santa Fe tracks and the Hangman Creek Valley. As a youngster, I could listen to the big

PERMITS/CONTACT
None required/Friends of the Bluff, www.friendsofthebluff.org

MAPS
USGS Spokane SW; city map

TRAIL NOTES
Leashed dogs OK; bikes welcome

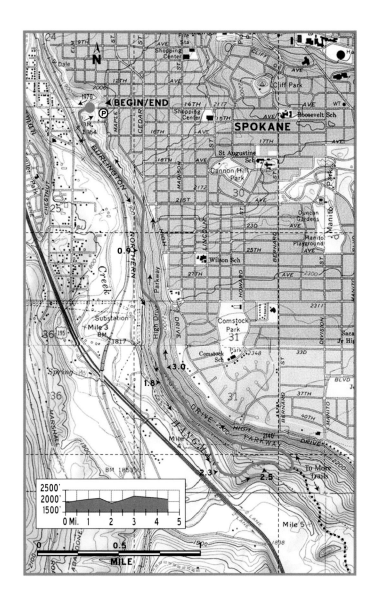

Hangman Creek flows at the bottom of the South Hill bluff

articulated steam locomotives more than a mile away, chugging up the hill to the city. Kids today can listen to the whine of diesel engines pulling that same hill.

A number of trailheads are available on this hike; I chose Polly Judd Park because it is closest to downtown Spokane. Pick up the trail as it drops to the south from the park and begins a long traverse above the railroad tracks and Hangman Creek below. The bluff grows increasingly higher as you walk to the south, offering numerous choices for trails along the way. Almost all of them interconnect and run south and north, so there's little danger of losing your way. To walk the route suggested here, try a gradually climbing traverse to keep equal distance between the top of the bluff along High Drive and the creek below.

At **0.9** mile, the route crosses under power lines and approaches a trail junction. Stay right at the junction and continue your climbing traverse, where traffic on US Route 195 can be noisy at times. In another mile, you'll cross under a second power line and look down upon a power substation where a juvenile—I'm not naming names—who didn't know any better rolled rocks down a gully toward it. Turn right at the next junction, about **1.8** miles from the trailhead, and descend to a flat shelf above the creek, where a pine forest slightly muffles highway noise.

At **2.3** miles, the path turns uphill and climbs steeply 200 vertical feet around a slide area, crossing under another power line **2.5** miles from the trailhead. Just beyond, you'll arrive at a trail fork and turn left, looping to the north and traversing along the bluff back toward your starting point. The route follows a 2,000-foot contour for a half-mile, where at **3.0** miles, you'll close the loop and retrace your steps 1.5 miles to the trailhead.

Going Farther

You can continue southeast for about 2 miles along the bluff, keeping above the creek and Qualchan Golf Course. Trailheads above are located along High Drive at 29th, 37th, and 57th Avenues and at Manito Boulevard. ■

SOUTHWEST SPOKANE

Columbia Plateau Trail, Fish Lake–Cheney

RATING	DISTANCE	HIKING TIME
★★★★☆	8.2 miles round-trip	4.5 hours

ELEVATION GAIN	HIGH POINT	DIFFICULTY
170 feet	2,350 feet	♦♦♦♦♦

BEST MONTHS
Jan Feb Mar **Apr May Jun Jul Aug Sep Oct** Nov Dec

The Hike

Walk the paved trail leading from Fish Lake Regional Park through forest and farmland to Cheney, home of the Eastern Washington University Eagles.

Getting There

Take Interstate 90 west to exit 270 and follow State Route 904 for 5.6 miles south to Cheney. Turn left on Cheney-Spokane Road and drive 2.9 miles to Fish Lake Regional Park, on the right. The parking lot, 2,180 feet above sea level, was free in 2017 and is just west of the Columbia Plateau State Park Trail, where you'll need a Discover Pass. If you've chosen to park here, follow a gravel road northeast up a hill to Columbia Plateau State Park Trail and take the paved trail south.

PERMITS/CONTACT
None (or Discover Pass)/Spokane County Parks and Recreation,
(509) 477-4730, www.spokanecounty.org/parks

MAPS
USGS Spokane SW; city map

TRAIL NOTES
Leashed dogs OK; bikes welcome;
respect private property by staying on the trail

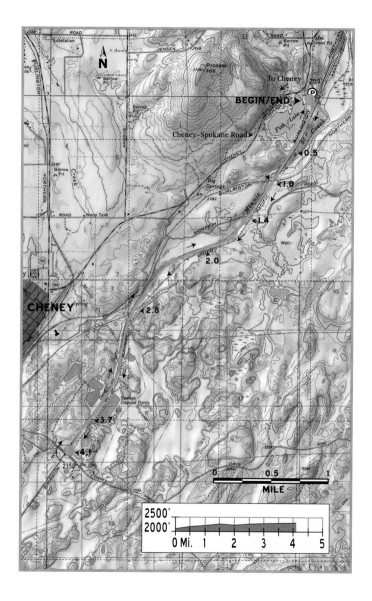

A bald eagle rests in a pine

A Spokane Transit Authority bus route serves Cheney and is less than a mile from the Cheney alternate trailhead for this hike. Call (509) 328-RIDE or visit SpokaneTransit.com.

The Trail
Probably because the paved portion of the Columbia Plateau State Park Trail beginning at Fish Lake is a little more than 4 miles one-way, it's not as popular with fast-moving road bicyclists as the longer Fish Lake Trail (Hike 2). That won't always be the case, as plans call for connecting the two trails in the future.

Start by hiking south along this splendid route above Fish Lake, carved by a massive ice age flood and a good spot to cool off after a summer hike and picnic, or try to catch a wily trout in the lake. It's an excellent spot to begin a family hike. You'll walk above the lake, passing interpretive signs and benches, for 0.5 mile.

The route then enters a long cut in the basalt rocks closing in on either side of the trail and reaching as high as 15 to 25 feet above the path. Thus your view is limited to looking along the rail corridor to the south—but that's not a bad thing, as a small stream flows along the man-made canyon in spring and early summer, filled with wildflowers and lined with pine trees where you might see eagles or hawks roosting. At **1.0** mile, the trail dives under the BNSF Railroad and at **1.4** miles, crosses under Anderson Road. Look up here, where a colony of barn swallows has taken up residence.

Beyond, the route begins to climb ever so slightly into pastureland on either side, **2.0** miles from the trailhead. Walk another 0.8 mile to a railroad overpass and turn farther south at a wide bend where flood-carved ponds litter the landscape and winged wildlife flourishes. At **3.7** miles, find what in summer will likely be a very welcome water stop and thank the good people of Cheney that the source is not the municipal sewage disposal site to the east.

Just beyond, **4.1** miles from the trailhead, pass under Cheney-Spangle Road and climb to the Cheney Trailhead, your turnaround point, on the left, where you'll find restrooms and picnic tables.

Going Farther

You can extend your hike by following the Columbia Plateau State Park Trail south for more than 30 miles (Hikes 6, 10, and 11), although the route is no longer paved. ∎

6. Columbia Plateau Trail, Cheney–Long Lake

RATING	DISTANCE	HIKING TIME
★★★★☆	7.0 miles round-trip	4 hours

ELEVATION GAIN	HIGH POINT	DIFFICULTY
80 feet	2,410 feet	♦♦♦♦♦

BEST MONTHS
Jan Feb Mar **Apr May** Jun Jul Aug **Sep Oct** Nov Dec

The Hike

Here's an excellent, easy trek along a rail trail that enters a sage and pine land dotted with lakes, leading to the Turnbull National Wildlife Refuge.

Getting There

Take Interstate 90 west to exit 270 and follow State Route 904 for 5.6 miles south to Cheney. Turn left on Cheney-Spangle Road and drive south 0.9 mile to the trailhead on the left, 2,330 feet above sea level. This trailhead, with its picnic tables and restrooms, serves as an alternate to the Fish Lake trailhead (Hike 2).

A Spokane Transit Authority bus route serves Cheney and is less than a mile from the trailhead. Call (509) 328-RIDE or visit SpokaneTransit.com.

PERMITS/CONTACT
Discover Pass required/Columbia Plateau State Park Trail, (509) 646-9218, www.parks.wa.gov

MAPS
USGS Amber; state park map

TRAIL NOTES
Leashed dogs OK; bikes and equestrians welcome (gravel/ballast surface); respect private property by staying on the trail

---

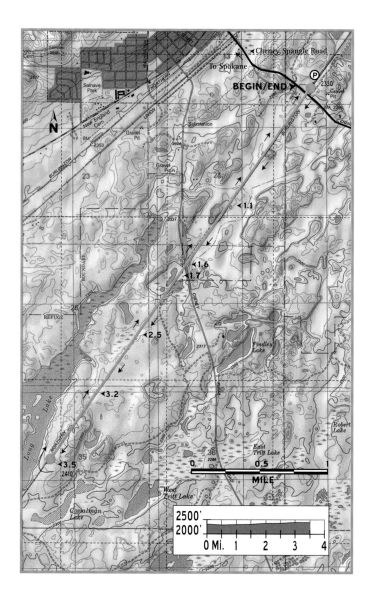

Fields turn pink in spring near Long Lake

The Trail

Straight as a printer's rule and level as a pancake griddle, this 3.5-mile section of the 130-mile-long Columbia Plateau State Park Trail is a gift to hikers, bicyclists, and equestrians from the old Spokane, Portland, and Seattle Railway. Plan your hike in the spring or fall rather than summer or winter—unless you like baking yourself or want to get in some cross-country skiing or snowshoeing.

Begin by following the paved path down to the trail that passes underneath Cheney-Spangle Road, then turn left on the trail where the pavement ends. Walk south along the old rail corridor in a flatland littered with low basalt outcrops and distant pine trees. At **1.1** miles, you'll walk through a cut in the rock to see farmhouses to the west and pastureland to the east. Distant train whistles might remind you of the heritage of this path.

At **1.6** miles, the route passes under Cheney-Plaza Road and immediately enters the Turnbull National Wildlife Refuge. It's a land of granddaddy ponderosa pines, lakes teeming with birds, herds of elk, and grumpy moose. This route through the refuge is the only one where you needn't pay an entry fee.

The trail continues to the southeast, passing between the first of many lakes in the refuge, **1.7** miles from the trailhead. Once past, pine trees line either side of the route at **2.4** miles, and wind through the needles plays a hushed tune. You'll find a bench at **2.5** miles, which might make a good turnaround spot for families with younger children.

Beyond, the route nears Long Lake at **3.2** miles, where you might spot wildlife with wings or hooves, and arrives at a good viewpoint of the lake at **3.5** miles. This is your turnaround spot.

Going Farther

You can continue your hike along the Columbia Plateau State Park Trail for another 4.5 miles to the Amber Lake Trailhead. If you're hiking with another party, consider a one-way walk of 8.0 miles with a key exchange. ■

7. Slavin Lake

RATING	DISTANCE	HIKING TIME
★★☆☆☆	5.8 miles round-trip	3 hours
ELEVATION GAIN	**HIGH POINT**	**DIFFICULTY**
340 feet	2,420 feet	◆◆◇◇◇
BEST MONTHS		
Jan Feb Mar Apr May Jun Jul Aug Sep Oct Nov Dec		

The Hike

A favorite among local birders, this sometimes soggy walk leads along wetlands and rocky plateaus where elk often can be seen with calves in the spring.

Getting There

Take Interstate 90 west to exit 279, follow US Route 195 south for more than 8 miles to Washington Road, and turn right. Drive a half-mile to Keeney Road and turn right, then immediately left into the James T. Slavin Conservation Area parking lot and trailhead, 2,340 feet above sea level, where you'll find a restroom.

PERMITS/CONTACT
None required/Spokane County Parks and Recreation
(509) 477-4730, www.spokanecounty.org/parks

MAPS
USGS Spokane SW; county map

TRAIL NOTES
Leashed dogs OK; equestrians welcome

The Trail

As you begin this hike by walking through meadows to the west, say a silent thank-you to the late James T. Slavin, who sold his 600-plus-acre farm to Spokane County Conservation Futures in 2000. Since that time, volunteers from a number of organizations including Spokane Mountaineers, Backcountry Horsemen of Washington, and Ducks Unlimited have helped the county turn the property into a place where you and I can stroll through big pines to a haven for feet featuring both webs and hooves.

Turn left at the first trail leading southwest and follow it for 0.7 mile, turning left at a junction and walking through a grove of aspen trees underneath a rocky cliff band. At **1.0** mile, take the gravel road leading to the right, an extension of Diamond Lane, and follow it to a path heading south in 0.1 mile. The route now leads southwest along the soggy edge of Slavin Lake, on the right, then curves and climbs to higher ground. Stay right at a trail junction at **1.3** miles, which you'll be taking on the return, before dropping down to a dike crossing the outlet of the lake, **1.5** miles from the trailhead.

Cross the dike, where in summer you might benefit from a machete to clear a path through shoulder-high grass and hidden snakes—which your correspondent is happy to report are not of the rattling variety—that slither hither and yon at your feet. Climb into more arid country on the other side of the dike and turn right at a trail junction at **1.8** miles. From here, the path leads north above the lake, with views through big old pines.

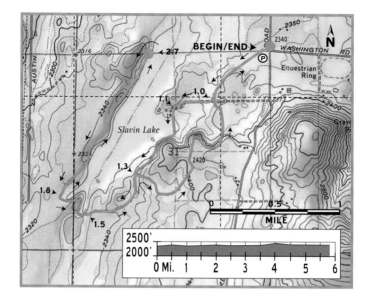

You can hike a short mile to a spot where the pathway drops back down toward the lake and enters tall grasses. A fence line here marks your turnaround spot, **2.7** miles from the trailhead.

Retrace your steps to the trail junction beyond the dike and turn right, climbing through a pine forest along rocky benches. Look to the trunks of large pines to the left of the trail for signs marking the graves of Slavin family pets before crossing a basalt plateau and dropping along a ledge to rejoin your entrance trail, 1.0 mile from the trailhead.

Going Farther

Several pathways weave through the conservation area, with the longest roughly circumnavigating the 638 acres for a hike of about 7.4 miles. ◼

8. Stubblefield Lake Loop

RATING	DISTANCE	HIKING TIME
★★★★☆	6.5 miles round-trip	4 hours

ELEVATION GAIN	HIGH POINT	DIFFICULTY
375 feet	2,380 feet	◆◆◆◆◆

BEST MONTHS
Jan Feb Mar Apr May Jun Jul Aug Sep Oct Nov Dec

The Hike

This is one of the best ways to see all that the Turnbull National Wildlife Refuge has to offer, from lakes and pine forests to coyotes and moose to geese and swans.

Getting There

Take Interstate 90 west to exit 270 and follow State Route 904 for 5.6 miles south to Cheney. Drive through town to Cheney-Plaza Road and turn left. Follow Cheney-Plaza Road for 4.2 miles to Smith Road and the entrance to Turnbull National Wildlife Refuge, and turn left. A self-pay registration station is located at the entrance ($3 per car in 2017; free November to February). The refuge is open from 6 a.m. to 9 p.m. during the summer and closes at 6 p.m. during the winter. Drive to the headquarters parking area and trailhead at 2,250 feet, where you'll also find restrooms.

PERMITS/CONTACT
Parking pass required/Turnbull National Wildlife Refuge,
(509) 235-4723, www.fws.gov/refuge/turnbull

MAPS
USGS Cheney; refuge brochure map or online

TRAIL NOTES
Leashed dogs OK; don't forget your binoculars and
long camera lenses!

The Trail

The Turnbull National Wildlife Refuge serves up more than 18,000 acres of wildlands and unlimited opportunities for getting up close and personal with 200 species of birds, including trumpeter swans; 45 species of mammals, such as Rocky Mountain elk and moose; and no less than 51 different kinds of butterflies. All of this on lands that are called—inappropriately, in

Hiking the Stubblefield Trail

my opinion—"channeled scablands." There's nothing scabby about Turnbull's beauty, aesthetically or in its purpose for being.

Judge for yourself. Walk south on the wide Headquarters Trail from the parking area, passing Headquarters Pond on your left and Winslow Pool on the right. At **0.9** mile, the wide gravel path forks at the Stubblefield Trail, your return route. Stay right for now and climb along a low bluff overlooking Cheever Lake on the right. At the south end of the lake, the Stubblefield Trail turns uphill to the left—but turn right first to a flood-control gate that overlooks Cheever Lake. This is a good spot, **1.6** miles from the trailhead, to scan the lake for winged and four-footed wildlife, especially in the early morning or evening. We spotted trumpeter swans at the north end of the lake, which tested (and flunked) the telephoto lenses on our cameras.

When you've exhausted the pixels on your smartphone or camera, walk back to the trail junction and stroll east along the refuge boundary in ponderosa pine forest, which diminishes as you follow the road, **2.7** miles from the trailhead. Continue another 0.7 mile to a junction with the boundary road and follow the trail to the left. You'll climb a low hill to the northeast and pass a viewpoint

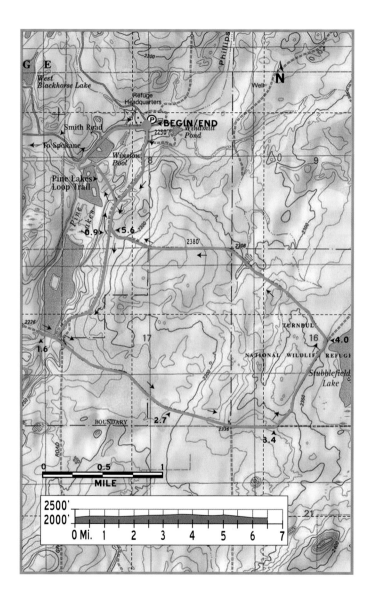

Swans at Turnbull National Wildlife Refuge

of Stubblefield Lake to the east, arriving at a second junction above the lake at **4.0** miles.

Turn left here and climb along rocky, open hills before descending into a narrow marshy draw, then climb over a barren hill before dropping down to join your return path, **5.6** miles from the trailhead. Turn right and walk down to the Pine Lakes Loop Trail on your left. Follow it downhill, turning right at the first junction and crossing the isthmus between Pine Lake on the left and Winslow Pool on the right, where there's an observation blind. This portion of the trail is paved and makes an excellent choice for hikers on wheels—though the short hill climb to the entrance road might require some assistance.

Turn right at the entrance road and walk the paved pathway back to the parking area at **6.5** miles. A trail with interpretive signs here also leads to Headquarters Pond. ■

9. Bluebird Trail

RATING	DISTANCE	HIKING TIME
★★★☆☆	5.2 miles round-trip	3 hours

ELEVATION GAIN	HIGH POINT	DIFFICULTY
150 feet	2,320 feet	◆◇◇◇◇

BEST MONTHS											
Jan	Feb	Mar	**Apr**	**May**	**Jun**	**Jul**	**Aug**	**Sep**	**Oct**	Nov	Dec

The Hike

Walk through ponderosa pine forest—a favorite with western bluebirds—to one of the larger lakes in the Turnbull National Wildlife Refuge before returning along an auto tour road.

Getting There

Take Interstate 90 west to exit 270 and follow State Route 904 for 5.6 miles south to Cheney. Drive through town to Cheney-Plaza Road and turn left. Follow Cheney-Plaza Road for 4.2 miles to Smith Road and the entrance to Turnbull National Wildlife Refuge, and turn left. A self-pay registration station is located at the entrance ($3 per car in 2017; free November to February). The refuge is open from 6 a.m. to 9 p.m. during the summer and closes at 6 p.m. during the winter. Drive to the headquarters parking area and trailhead at 2,250 feet, where you'll also find restrooms.

PERMITS/CONTACT
Parking pass required/Turnbull National Wildlife Refuge,
(509) 235-4723, www.fws.gov/refuge/turnbull

MAPS
USGS Cheney; refuge brochure map or online

TRAIL NOTES
Leashed dogs OK; don't forget your binoculars and
long camera lenses!

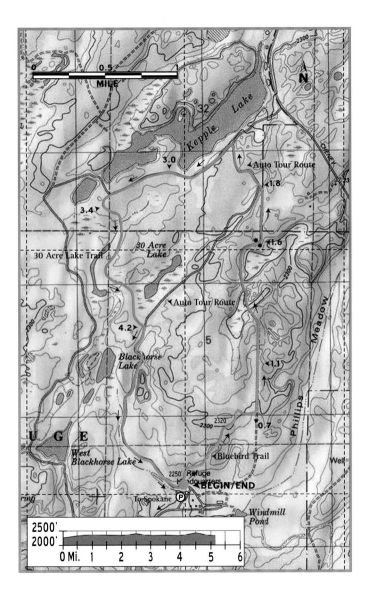

0   0.5   1
MILE

N

Kepple Lake

32

3.0

◄Auto Tour Route

◄1.8

3.4▼

•◄1.6

30 Acre Lake Trail

30 Acre Lake

◄Auto Tour Route

4.2▼

5

◄1.1

R E F U G E

2320
2300

►0.7

Phillips Meadow

Cheney

U G E

West Blackhorse Lake ◄

Blackhorse Lake

◄Bluebird Trail

Well

2250' Refuge Headquarters

◄BEGIN/END

To Spokane Ⓟ

Windmill Pond

2500'
2000'

0 Mi.   1   2   3   4   5   6

Kepple Lake is a major attraction for birders along the Bluebird Trail loop

The Trail

Plan to take this hike in the early morning or evening, when you have the best chances to see the wildlife to which this refuge is dedicated. To see the largest variety, try this hike during migration periods, from mid-March to mid-May or September through October. Quaking aspen make for splendid colors in the fall.

Find the Bluebird Trail, which leads northeast up a gradual hill into a pine forest and crosses a clearing before joining a road along a power line, **0.7** mile from the trailhead. Turn left and follow the rocky road north for a short half-mile to a wide pathway and smoother surface at **1.1** miles. Return to the power line and a gate at **1.6** miles, walk a short quarter-mile, and join a road that is part of the Pine Creek Auto Tour Route, **1.8** miles from the trailhead.

Turn right and follow the auto route north to the Kepple Lake parking area, and turn right along the road closed to auto traffic. User pathways lead to several spots overlooking the lake, which is a haven to many of the 124 species of birds that nest in the refuge. You can walk about 0.3 mile before turning around at the refuge boundary and returning to the Kepple Lake parking area.

Now walk the auto tour road to the southwest to restrooms and the paved Kepple Peninsula Interpretive Trail at **3.0** miles, a good stop for outdoorsfolk who do their hiking in wheelchairs. The path leads around the peninsula to interpretive signs and an observation blind. Returning to the auto road—bicyclists enjoy this 5.5-mile loop as well—turn right and walk to the 30-Acre Lake hiking trail, **3.4** miles from the trailhead.

Turn left here, and follow the trail along a marshy pond to the west and the southern end of 30-Acre Lake, which (spoiler alert) spans about 30 acres. You'll rejoin the auto tour route at **4.2** miles, pass a restroom at the Blackhorse Lake loop trail, and return to the trailhead at **5.2** miles. The auto tour route is one-way, and you'll be facing oncoming traffic on your return. ■

10. Columbia Plateau Trail, Downs Lake North

RATING ★★☆☆☆	DISTANCE 8.0 miles round-trip	HIKING TIME 4.5 hours
ELEVATION GAIN 100 feet	HIGH POINT 2,150 feet	DIFFICULTY ♦♦◇◇◇
BEST MONTHS Jan Feb Mar **Apr May** Jun Jul Aug **Sep Oct** Nov Dec		

The Hike
Follow the Columbia Plateau State Park Trail north along a marshy lake through arid sage land and basalt formations decorated by springtime wildflowers.

Getting There
Take Interstate 90 west to exit 270 and follow State Route 904 for 8.3 miles south through Cheney to Mullinix Road. Turn left on Mullinix, which becomes Martin Road, and drive 21.2 miles to the

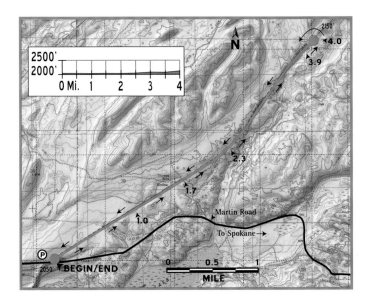

Martin Road Trailhead on the right, 2,050 feet above sea level, where you'll find restrooms and trail information.

The Trail

This is the hottest and driest part of the Columbia Plateau State Park Trail you'll find described in this guide, and therefore provides

---

PERMITS/CONTACT
Discover Pass required/Columbia Plateau State Park Trail, (509) 646-9218, www.parks.wa.gov

MAPS
USGS Fishtrap Lake; state park map

TRAIL NOTES
Leashed dogs OK; bikes and equestrians welcome (gravel/ballast surface); respect private property by staying on the trail

A cyclist rides the ballast of the Columbia Plateau State Park Trail near Downs Lake

a good opportunity to stretch your hiking muscles in the spring, when wildlife and wildflower watching is best.

The route heads northwest along a plateau above marshy Downs Lake to the south along barren sage land punctuated by basalt outcrops and mini-mesas. You'll hike about a mile before encountering anything resembling a tree and another 0.7 mile before crossing rural Falk Road and a homesite and the old railroad wayside at Rodna.

At **2.3** miles from the trailhead, the way passes a stand of aspen in a draw to the southeast, where you might find deer seeking shade. Red-tailed hawks cruise the sky looking for a mouse meal, and legless critters like lizards and rattlesnakes hobnob in the sun. Meadowlarks warble and killdeer pretend they've broken their wings to lead you from babies in the nest.

At **3.9** miles, you'll pass through a draw that is often wet in the spring and one of the few spots that stays green through the early summer. A corridor sliced through the basalt at **4.0** miles is your turn-around spot. ■

11. Columbia Plateau Trail, Amber Lake North

RATING	DISTANCE	HIKING TIME
★★★☆☆	6.8 miles round-trip	3.5 hours
ELEVATION GAIN	HIGH POINT	DIFFICULTY
100 feet	2,300 feet	◆◆◆◆◆

BEST MONTHS
Jan Feb Mar **Apr May** Jun Jul Aug **Sep Oct** Nov Dec

The Hike

This trek takes you north and east along a rock-rimmed lake and open prairie to welcome shade in the pines.

Getting There

Take Interstate 90 west to exit 270 and follow State Route 904 for 8.3 miles south through Cheney to Mullinix Road. Turn left on Mullinix, drive 9.5 miles to Pine Springs Road, and turn right. Drive 1.4 miles to the Amber Lake trailhead on the left, 2,300 feet above sea level, where you'll find a restroom. You'll share the large parking area with anglers and boat trailer parking.

The Trail

Things can be pretty warm during the summer months and windy pretty much any time of the year, but don't let either of these small

---

PERMITS/CONTACT
Discover Pass required/Columbia Plateau State Park Trail, (509) 646-9218, www.parks.wa.gov

MAPS
USGS Amber; state park map

TRAIL NOTES
Leashed dogs OK; bikes and equestrians welcome (gravel/ballast surface); respect private property by staying on the trail

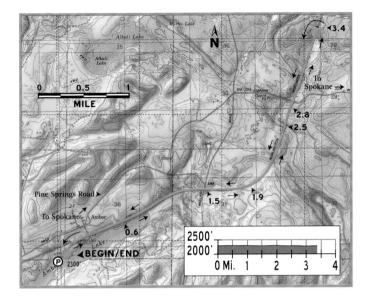

matters deter you from taking this easy walk. You'll be rewarded with wildlife sightings along Amber Lake both in the air and on the water.

Begin by climbing a bank to the old railroad grade to the east, turning right and passing a private residence before crossing the trailhead road. At **0.6** mile, you'll find a good view of the lake below and a bench that might make a welcome rest stop on your return. You'll follow above the lakeshore for a bit before entering a pine forest at **1.0** mile, where you might spot deer in the shade of the trees.

At **1.5** miles, you'll walk under a huge metal culvert where Mullinix Road crosses above, and emerge to the sound of aspen trees rustling in the wind. Prairie and pastureland await beyond, following the trail corridor bounded by cattails and willows before beginning a wide turn to the north, **1.9** miles from the trailhead.

After about a mile, the view opens to the north and a line of pine trees mark a shadier stretch of the route, **2.5** miles from the trailhead. In another 0.3 mile, cross the gravel Sterling Road and follow the trail another 0.6 mile to your turn-around spot, **3.4** miles from the trailhead.

Going Farther
You can stretch this hike as far north as you wish. It's a little more than 12 miles to the Cheney trailhead (described in Hike 6). If you're hiking with another party, consider a one-way walk with a key exchange. ■

Wetlands and sage along the trail

12. Hog Lake

RATING	DISTANCE	HIKING TIME
★★★☆☆	5.4 miles round-trip	3 hours

ELEVATION GAIN	HIGH POINT	DIFFICULTY
590 feet	2,190 feet	♦♦◇◇◇

BEST MONTHS
Jan Feb Mar **Apr May** Jun Jul Aug **Sep** Oct Nov Dec

The Hike
Wander along open, rocky scablands above a narrow canyon and lake to a seasonal waterfall.

Getting There
Drive west on Interstate 90 for about 26 miles to exit 254 and turn left on Sprague Highway. Drive about 2.4 miles to Scroggie Road at the Fishtrap Lake Resort sign and turn left. Drive a half-mile to a wide parking area and trailhead on the right, 2,150 feet above sea level.

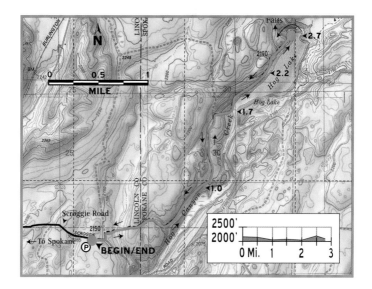

The Trail

This hike shares the Bureau of Land Management trailhead with Fishtrap Lake (Hike 13), and although the lakes are separated by less than two miles, Hog Lake is the preferred destination, if only because of the waterfall you'll see at its end. Don't wait too long into the spring to take this trek or the waterfall will be nothing more than a long gully filled with water-stained rocks.

PERMITS/CONTACT
None required/Bureau of Land Management, Spokane,
(509) 536-1200, www.blm.gov/contact/oregon-washington

MAPS
USGS Fishtrap; BLM map

TRAIL NOTES
Leashed dogs OK; bikes and equestrians welcome

Hog Lake stretches north from the boat launch

Begin by crossing Scroggie Road to the north and walking about 175 yards east along the road to a gate and twin-track pathway leading north. Find two gates leading downhill on the right and follow either one as the trails soon merge to descend into a gully before climbing past a second gate. Turn to the northeast as the trail meanders in the pine forest and cattle trails crisscross the main route, marked by flexible brown posts labeled TRAIL. I am not certain but believe the signs were placed here so as not to confuse the cows, which clearly ignore them.

At **1.0** mile, you'll pass above a green wetland on the right between rocky cliff bands above and below the pathway. The route strikes the southern end of Hog Lake at **1.7** miles and follows a road downhill to a boat launch. An angler trail leads along the shoreline, but eventually steep cliffs will encourage you to climb any of several trails uphill to a twin-track pathway that skirts a wet area and contours above the lake, **2.2** miles from the trailhead. You'll arrive at a rocky knoll above the lake with a view down to the falls at **2.7** miles. The falls are on private land, so enjoy them from a distance at this turn-around point. ∎

13. Fishtrap Lake

RATING	DISTANCE	HIKING TIME
★★☆☆☆	6.4 miles round-trip	3.5 hours
ELEVATION GAIN	**HIGH POINT**	**DIFFICULTY**
275 feet	2,150 feet	◆◇◇◇◇
BEST MONTHS		
Jan Feb Mar **Apr May** Jun Jul Aug **Sep Oct** Nov Dec		

The Hike

Walk through wild scablands and a partially burned pine forest to a picnic spot and lakeside plateau.

Getting There

Drive west on Interstate 90 for about 26 miles to exit 254 and turn left on Sprague Highway. Drive about 2.4 miles to Scroggie Road at the Fishtrap Lake Resort sign and turn left. Drive a half-mile to a wide parking area and trailhead on the right, 2,150 feet above sea level.

The Trail

This twin-track trail heads south through rock-strewn Bureau of Land Management prairie land, where you may share the trail with cattle and most certainly with cattle calling cards—massive whorls of dung that, when dried, make excellent recyclable golf discs (think chip-chucking). This country gets hot in the summer, especially since a 2014 brush fire scalded a number of shade-providing pines, so plan to hike in spring or fall.

PERMITS/CONTACT
None required/Bureau of Land Management, Spokane, (509) 536-1200, www.blm.gov/contact/oregon-washington

MAPS
USGS Fishtrap; BLM map

TRAIL NOTES
Leashed dogs OK; bikes and equestrians welcome

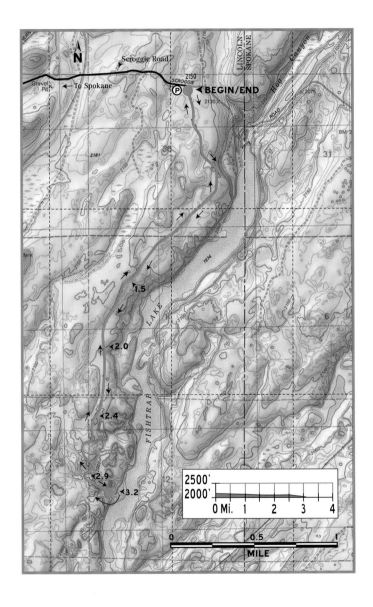

Begin by walking south through the gate and passing private property and a residence around its west side. Pick up the route on the other side as it alternately climbs and drops through the barren countryside. Fishtrap Lake, a popular angling destination in the spring, is hidden in a canyon on your left. Tall, flexible brown stakes labeled TRAIL mark the route here.

Fishtrap Lake in the distance

At **1.5** miles, the lake can be seen from a rise, and in another half-mile you'll arrive at a gate and fork in the path. Stay left and head through the gate, passing a pond on the right at **2.4** miles. In another half-mile, you'll drop down a rocky cliff band to a trail junction **2.9** miles from the trailhead.

Turn left in this wooded section untouched by fire and hike another 0.3 mile east to the lake. This area is named Farmer's Landing, a good spot for a picnic above the lake. Return the way you came.

Going Farther
You can add about 2 miles to this hike by heading west at the first trail junction and walking to a twin-track path leading north to the Bureau of Land Management ranch house, about 1 mile. Turn right and follow the trail back to your return trail at the gate, 2.0 miles from the trailhead, and turn left. ■

14. Towell Falls

RATING	DISTANCE	HIKING TIME
★☆☆☆☆	6.8 miles round-trip	4 hours

ELEVATION GAIN	HIGH POINT	DIFFICULTY
520 feet	1,580 feet	♦♦♦♦♦

BEST MONTHS
Jan Feb Mar **Apr May** Jun Jul Aug Sep **Oct Nov** Dec

The Hike

Views unencumbered by all but a few trees make this rangeland walk to a seasonal waterfall a good one for spotting coyotes, raptors, and other such critters.

Getting There

Take Interstate 90 west to exit 245 and drive through Sprague to Highway 23 southeast to Steptoe. Follow State Route 23 for about 12 miles to the gravel Davis Road and turn right. Follow Davis Road for nearly 7 miles to Jordan-Knott Road and turn left. Follow Jordan-Knott Road for 2.2 miles to the Rock Creek Management Area, turn right, and follow the road for 2.4 miles to the Escure Ranch picnic area on the right, 1,470 feet above sea level, where you'll find tables, a restroom, a corral, and a watering trough with welcome—but not potable—water.

> **PERMITS/CONTACT**
> None required/Bureau of Land Management, Spokane, (509) 536-1200, www.blm.gov/or/districts/spokane
>
> **MAPS**
> USGS Honn Lakes, USGS Revere; BLM map
>
> **TRAIL NOTES**
> Leashed dogs OK; bikes and equestrians welcome

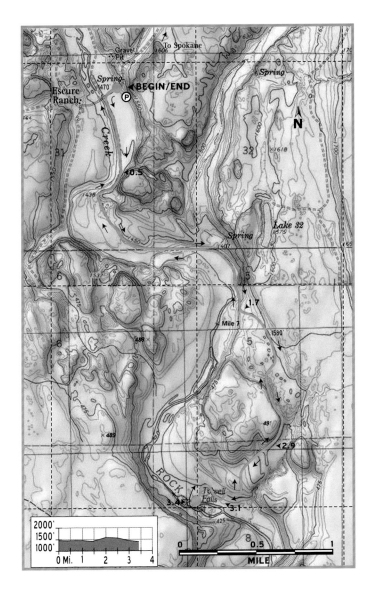

To Spokane

Gravel
Pit

Spring

Spring

BEGIN/END

Escure
Ranch

N

0.5

Creek

Lake 32

Spring

1.7

Mile 7

2.9

ROCK

Towell
Falls

3.4

3.1

2000'
1500'
1000'

0 Mi. 1 2 3 4

0 0.5 1

MILE

Towell Falls is barely a trickle in midsummer

The Trail

All but the last 0.3 mile of this hike are on a rough road best suited for high clearance or four-wheel-drive vehicles, which you'll seldom see unless you visit during hunting season. Don't wait too long into late spring to hike here; it can be incredibly hot and windy and there's scant shade along the way. Carry plenty of water, and keep an eye to the ground for rattlesnakes.

The road heads south above Rock Creek, which is difficult to reach because its banks are overgrown with tall grasses and brush. The path heads gently downhill, where the twin tracks might be covered with gravel ballast in spots and deep dust in others, to the only area shaded by trees, about **0.5** mile from the trailhead. At **1.7** miles, the road climbs a steep basalt plateau and circles around a low hill on the west, where you'll get a distant view of Towell Falls, **2.9** miles from the trailhead.

Continue down the road to a parking area at **3.1** miles, then circle a rocky depression to the northwest to a viewpoint of the falls at **3.4** miles, your turnaround point. The falls are barely a trickle by mid-July.

Going Farther

Old ranch roads can be followed north and west from the parking area to Wall, Turtle, and Perch Lakes, or along Rock Creek to the north. ∎

NORTHEAST SPOKANE

15. Palisades Park

RATING	DISTANCE	HIKING TIME
★★☆☆☆	**4.4 miles round-trip**	**2.5 hours**

ELEVATION GAIN	HIGH POINT	DIFFICULTY
460 feet	**2,190 feet**	◆◆◇◇◇

BEST MONTHS
Jan Feb Mar **Apr May Jun Jul Aug Sep Oct** Nov Dec

The Hike

Get a great view of the city and surrounding hills while hiking through pine forest past basalt canyons and towers.

Getting There

From Interstate 90, take exit 280 and follow Walnut Street north to 2nd Avenue. Turn left on 2nd, drive west, and bear left on Sunset Boulevard. Keep to the right of the underpass on Sunset Boulevard and cross the bridge over Latah Creek. At the first stoplight—Government Way—turn right and drive 0.8 mile, bearing left on Greenwood Road at a Y intersection. Follow Greenwood for 1 mile to the top of the hill and the big parking area on the left and a smaller one on the right, where you'll find the trailhead, 2,190 feet above sea level.

The Trail

Here is the first hike where we saw the blight caused by nonnative, invasive weeds. Once golden in the spring with native arrowleaf balsamroot, Palisades Park resembles a cultivated farmland of killer skeleton weed and knapweed—despite valiant removal efforts by Spokane City Parks and Recreation and volunteers who made this a hiker's gem. Parts of the trail are overgrown so much by the terrorist plants that by mid-June, the path becomes invisible.

If you've parked in the larger lot south of Greenwood, cross the road and find the trailhead and Trail 101, which heads north along the Palisades Park boundary for 0.7 mile. Here, you'll find a trail junction and turn left along the path, bounded on the left by a fence

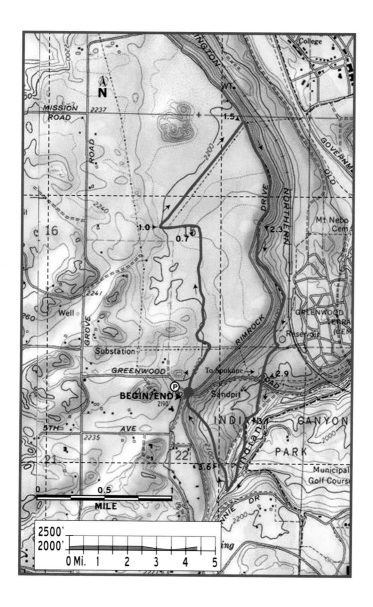

PERMITS/CONTACT
None required/Spokane City Parks and Recreation,
(509) 625-6200, www.spokaneparks.org

MAPS
USGS Spokane SW; city map

TRAIL NOTES
Leashed dogs OK; equestrians and bikes welcome

line. For a lesson in how grazing can control weeds, look at the clear pastureland to the west. Walk for 0.3 mile to the edge of the park and cross under a power line.

Just beyond, turn right on Trail 122, which roughly parallels the power line and a buried waterline that serves Fairchild Air Force Base. At **1.5** miles, you'll pass a pump station and join the old Rimrock Drive, once a prime auto tour. This section of the gravel road is now closed to traffic and leads south along Rimrock, volcanic basalt cliffs that drop nearly 100 vertical feet to the Greenwood Cemetery below. Turn right and walk the road, taking in the view of downtown Spokane and the hills beyond, including big, bald Mount Spokane.

At **2.2** miles, you'll cross a marvelous example of Civilian Conservation Corps handcrafting: an arched bridge over a narrow canyon. The best view of the bridge is from the south end. Continue south for about 200 feet to a path that drops sharply to the left and joins Trail 101. At **2.3** miles, stay right on a path that first drops and parallels railroad tracks below before climbing steeply back uphill. Keep to the right of a reservoir at **2.7** miles, and at **2.9** miles, cross Greenwood Road and look left to the wide pathway leading south into the thick pine forest.

Follow this old road for about a quarter-mile to a trail leading downhill to the left, **3.1** miles from the trailhead. The route now drops into Indian Canyon and crosses a creek before climbing to a junction with Trails 121 and 107 at **3.4** miles. Stay left and follow Trail 121 for 0.2 mile, passing a viewpoint of a nice waterfall. A way trail leads down into the canyon, passing a small cave in the basalt walls.

Spokane from Palisades Park

Stay above on the wide path as it curves around the head of the canyon and enters a wide meadow where the Spokane Tribe once camped, and turn left at a junction here, **3.6** miles from the trailhead. This section of the trail climbs through basalt outcrops to the parking area above.

Going Farther
A number of pathways can be walked to make interconnecting loops for another 2.0 miles in Palisades Park, with the largest a loop that circles the archery range below Rimrock. ■

16. Bowl and Pitcher Loop

RATING	DISTANCE	HIKING TIME
★★★☆☆	4.0 miles round-trip	2.5 hours

ELEVATION GAIN	HIGH POINT	DIFFICULTY
275 feet	1,875 feet	◆◆◆◇◇

BEST MONTHS
Jan Feb Mar **Apr May Jun** Jul Aug **Sep Oct** Nov Dec

The Hike

Visit one of Spokane's most prominent landmarks before trekking downriver past lumpy basalt outcrops and climbing to a plateau above the Spokane River.

Getting There

Take exit 280 from Interstate 90 in Spokane and follow Walnut Street north across the Maple Street Bridge to Francis Avenue. Turn left on Francis and follow it as it drops down and turns northwest, renamed Nine Mile Road and State Route 291. Turn left onto Rifle Club Road, where a sign points to Riverside State Park, and follow it west through a residential area to Aubrey White Parkway. Turn left on the parkway and enjoy the drive above the Spokane River for 1.3 miles to the entrance to the Bowl and Pitcher area and Riverside State Park Campground on the right. Follow the signs to the day-use area, where you'll find parking, the trailhead, and restrooms, 1,740 feet above sea level.

PERMITS/CONTACT
Discover Pass required/Riverside State Park, (509) 465-5064, www.parks.wa.gov

MAPS
USGS Spokane NW, USGS Airway Heights; state park map

TRAIL NOTES
Bikes and leashed dogs welcome

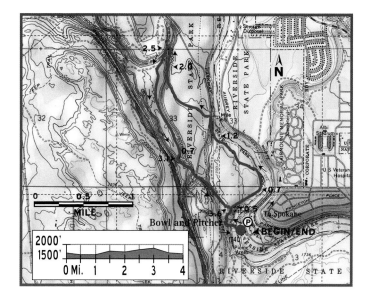

The Trail

This is another walk where it's easy to get confused by the number of trails and junctions, although most pathways are posted and numbered. Begin by walking the paved way leading down to the Swinging Bridge, which is wheelchair accessible with assistance. It takes a bit of stomping and jumping to get the bridge swinging, but it's a great spot to grab selfies of the whitewater tumbling over rapids downstream to the Bowl and Pitcher.

In what must be at least sixty-five years of trying, I've never been able to figure out why they named it the Bowl and Pitcher. I see a couple of very large lumps of basalt at the river's edge and with a stretch of imagination possibly make out a Colonial-style pitcher without a handle next to a very large lump of basalt. I'm certain you'll do much better.

Once you're all selfied and bounced, cross to the west side of the bridge and climb a few steps to Trail 25, **0.5** mile from the trailhead. Turn right and walk to the north between large basalt formations,

Arrowleaf balsamroot color the slopes

passing way trails that lead off toward the river. At **0.7** mile, you'll find a junction with Trail 211 and follow it straight ahead to a viewpoint of the Devil's Toenail rapid at **1.2** miles.

Beyond, the trail begins climbing toward a plateau on the left and emerges at **1.4** miles on the paved Centennial Trail. Cross it and continue on Trail 211 to a junction with Trail 200 at **2.0** miles. Trails along the plateau are favored by mountain bikers and equestrians and meander south through grassland for more than a mile. At **2.1** miles, take Trail 201 to the left and follow it to a junction with Trail 210. Stay left on 210, which climbs a bluff to the east to a fork and Trail 25, **2.5** miles from the trailhead.

Turn left on Trail 25 and climb north along a ridge crest to an upper plateau overlooking your route below. You'll see a way trail leading west to a steep hillside at **2.8** miles. This route leads to an abandoned railway grade that can be hiked for several miles, but unless you're looking for more exercise, continue straight ahead to a junction with Trail 210 at **3.1** miles. Turn left on Trail 210 and, if you're hiking in summer, welcome the shade and downgrade. You'll cross the paved Centennial Trail in another 0.1 mile and follow Trail 210 downhill to its junction with Trails 25 and 211, **3.6** miles from the trailhead. Follow Trails 25 and 211 to the right, cross the Swinging Bridge, and climb back to the trailhead at **4.0** miles.

Going Farther

For a rugged walk, take the abandoned railway grade to the northwest for a mile or so, returning the way you came. You can also extend this hike by continuing either south or north on Trail 25 or the Centennial Trail.

Riverside State Park has an excellent campground with both RV and tent sites, including some popular sites fronting the Spokane River. It's often full during summer months, but an alternative summer campground is about 7 miles south at Lake Spokane. Cross the Nine Mile Falls Dam and follow Charles Road to the campground entrance. ■

17. Bowl and Pitcher Upriver

RATING ★★★★	DISTANCE 6.0 miles round-trip	HIKING TIME 3.5 hours
ELEVATION GAIN 225 feet	HIGH POINT 1,780 feet	DIFFICULTY ♦♦
BEST MONTHS Jan Feb Mar Apr May Jun Jul Aug Sep Oct Nov Dec		

The Hike

Walk along a shaded trail following the Spokane River upstream from the landmark Bowl and Pitcher to a beach and picnic site along the water.

Getting There

Take exit 280 from Interstate 90 in Spokane and follow Walnut Street north across the Maple Street Bridge to Francis Avenue. Turn left on

PERMITS/CONTACT
Discover Pass required/Riverside State Park, (509) 465-5064,
www.parks.wa.gov

MAPS
USGS Spokane NW; state park map

TRAIL NOTES
Bikes and leashed dogs welcome; popular equestrian area

Francis and follow it as it drops down and turns northwest, renamed Nine Mile Road and State Route 291. Turn left onto Rifle Club Road, where a sign points to Riverside State Park, and follow it west through a residential area to Aubrey White Parkway. Turn left on the parkway and enjoy the drive above the Spokane River for 1.3 miles to the entrance of the Bowl and Pitcher area and Riverside State Park Campground on the right. Follow the signs to the day-use area, where you'll find parking, the trailhead, and restrooms, 1,740 feet above sea level.

The Trail

My infinitely better half, B. B. Hardbody, agrees with me—which is more than a rarity—that this is the best hike from the Bowl and Pitcher. The main reason is that about three-quarters of the trail is sheltered from the hot summer sun by big pines, which means a cooler walk. And in late summer, you can actually wade or even swim in a river eddy where the current isn't as dangerous as it is early in the season.

Start with a trek down the paved trail to the Swinging Bridge, which is navigable by wheelchairs with assistance. In 1997, this bridge replaced the original 216-foot Civilian Conservation Corps suspension bridge that was finished in 1940. It gives you a great view of the roiling Spokane River both downstream, to the Bowl and Pitcher, and upstream, where you might see terrified tourists headed toward one of its most rugged whitewater-rafting sections.

After crossing the bridge, climb the stairs and turn left on Trail 25 as it traverses above the river, and pass several user trails on the right.

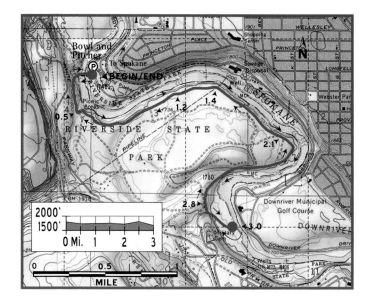

At **0.5** mile, you'll enter a small meadow and a path leading to a rock viewpoint overlooking the river and Swinging Bridge. Return to the main Trail 25 and stay left at the next junction. At **1.2** miles, turn left on Trail 100 as it follows the curve of the river. Stay to the left from this point along the river on Trail 100 as you pass a number of user trails.

At **1.4** miles, you'll hike past the Spokane sewage treatment plant, which is on the opposite bank of the river. It's remarkable that the aroma isn't nearly as bad as you might imagine. Continue upriver, staying left at all junctions, and at **2.1** miles, you'll find yourself walking along the river's edge. From here, traverse uphill along a steep, open hillside to a trail junction at **2.8** miles.

To the right is a bench overlooking the river and the paved Centennial Trail. Look to the left to find a way trail leading down to a broad, brushy meadow and beach, your turnaround spot at **3.0** miles. This area is often flooded in the early spring; if so, that bench is a comfortable place to watch the river roll past.

Lupine and arrowleaf balsamroot

Going Farther

You can combine this hike with any of the downriver trails, such as Trail 25 (Hike 16), or follow the Centennial Trail to the south for about 2.0 miles to the T. J. Meenach Bridge and Spokane Falls Community College.

Riverside State Park has an excellent campground with both RV and tent sites, including some popular sites fronting the Spokane River. It's often full during summer months, but an alternative summer campground is about 7 miles south at Lake Spokane. Cross the Nine Mile Falls Dam and follow Charles Road to the campground entrance. ∎

18. Indian Painted Rocks

RATING	DISTANCE	HIKING TIME
★★☆☆☆	3.6 miles round-trip	2.5 hours

ELEVATION GAIN	HIGH POINT	DIFFICULTY
175 feet	1,635 feet	♦◇◇◇◇

BEST MONTHS
Jan Feb **Mar Apr May Jun Jul Aug Sep Oct Nov** Dec

The Hike

This pleasant family walk along the Little Spokane River passes rocks painted by ancient Native Americans and is a favorite of birders and wildlife watchers.

Getting There

Take exit 280 from Interstate 90 in Spokane and follow Walnut Street north across the Maple Street Bridge to Francis Avenue. Turn left on Francis, drive west to Indian Trail Road, and turn right. Head north on Indian Trail Road for 4.7 miles to Rutter Parkway and continue straight on Rutter Parkway, following sharp downhill curves to a bridge crossing the Little Spokane River. Turn left into the parking area just past the bridge, where you'll find a restroom. The trailhead, 1,580 feet above sea level, is at the west end of the parking area.

The Trail

Less than 6 miles from the Spokane city limits, the hike past Indian Painted Rocks is a popular put-in spot for paddlers as well as a trailhead for hikers looking to spot everything from bald eagles to moose. So expect the parking area to get a bit crowded on summer weekends.

You'll find a side trail leading right to the painted rocks just beyond the trailhead. After vandals defaced the paintings, Washington State Park officials put the rocks behind bars, where the paintings remain faintly visible.

The trail follows the Little Spokane downriver, circumnavigating the wetlands a few hundred yards from the main stream channel. Look in these reedy areas for deer and the occasional moose as you walk through a section of pine forest destroyed by fire in 2015. At **0.5** mile, the trail passes close to the stream, where in late spring, you might get a glimpse of the thousands of yellow irises growing wild along its banks.

Beyond, the trail turns right at a wood barrier meant to keep pedestrians from following the faint river trail into heron nesting and roosting territory. The route now climbs across a glacier-polished granite slab that youngsters (and the occasional old waddler who still thinks he can rely on friction) will delight in scrambling upon. The path then turns into a wide gully and climbs at a moderate pace to a bench and view down to the river, **0.9** mile from the trailhead.

Oregon grape

Drop into the gully, then climb back to another viewpoint and traverse along the hillside. The pines here

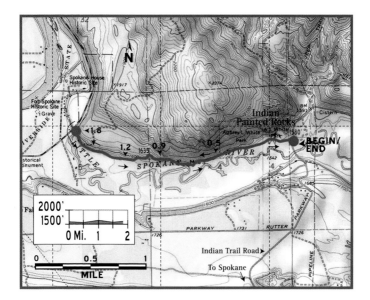

escaped the wildfire and offer some cooling shade in the summer, and the path now drops at a moderate pace to the river flats, **1.2** miles from the trailhead.

Here's another section where you're likely to see deer and other critters with hooves in the tall grasses toward the river. Massive ponderosa pines decorate the hillside to the north and scatter cones on the twin-tracked trail. The route climbs to **1.8** miles at paved North River Park Lane and ends at an alternate trailhead and parking area off State Route 291, your turnaround point.

Going Farther

To extend your hike, follow the marked path that climbs north from the North River Park Lane trailhead along the Knothead Loop (Hike 19), which adds a 3-mile loop to your trip. ■

19. Knothead Loop

RATING	DISTANCE	HIKING TIME
★★★★☆	6.6 miles round-trip	4 hours

ELEVATION GAIN	HIGH POINT	DIFFICULTY
985 feet	2,482 feet	◆ ◆ ◆ ◇ ◇

BEST MONTHS
Jan Feb Mar **Apr May Jun Jul Aug Sep Oct Nov** Dec

The Hike

Take this fine trek to see wildflowers in the spring and wildlife any time of the year while getting a good workout climbing to great views of the Spokane River.

Getting There

Take exit 280 from Interstate 90 in Spokane and follow Walnut Street north across the Maple Street Bridge to Francis Avenue. Turn left on Francis, drive west to Indian Trail Road, and turn right. Head north on Indian Trail Road for 4.7 miles to Rutter Parkway and continue straight, following sharp downhill curves to a bridge crossing the Little Spokane River. Turn left into the parking area just past the bridge, where you'll find a restroom. The trailhead, 1,580 feet above sea level, is at the northeast end of the parking area near the restroom.

The Trail

You won't find a better hike closer to the city, made even finer by those good volunteers of the Washington Trails Association and staff of Washington State Parks, who have been working to reroute private property portions of the path onto park land. Sightings of deer, moose, birds of prey, and wild turkeys are frequent; wood ticks are plentiful in the spring and summer. In good snow years—and folks around here consider a snow year as "good" if there's enough white stuff to make a snow angel at least 8 inches deep—expect to see snowshoe hikers and possibly cross-country skiers along the trail.

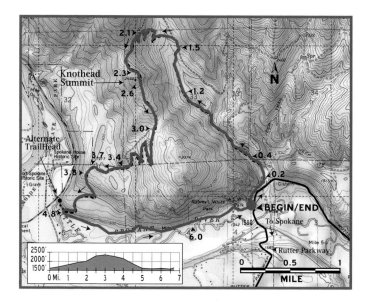

Begin by climbing northeast over a rocky hump in pine forest blackened by a 2015 wildfire, then descending to a trailhead sign and twin-track path leading north into the burned area, **0.2** mile from the trailhead. This section appears to have been bulldozed during the fire, which kept most of the destruction to the west of the route.

The way leads up a wide, gentle valley into a broad gully where basalt outcrops to the west were exposed by the fire. At **0.4** mile, the blaze turned away up the hillside to the west, and you'll enter the

PERMITS/CONTACT
Discover Pass required/Riverside State Park, (509) 465-5064, www.parks.wa.gov

MAPS
USGS Nine Mile Falls, USGS Dartford; state park map

TRAIL NOTES
Bikes and pets prohibited in the Little Spokane Natural Area

The summit of the Knothead trail affords a good view of the Spokane River

pinewood on either side of the route. The valley floor is decorated in the early spring by flowering serviceberry and—a surprise to at least one old waddler—several yellow fawn lilies.

The wide draw grows increasingly narrow and slightly steeper before turning northerly into a wider valley decorated by pine trees **1.2** miles from the trailhead. The route continues a gentle climb for another 0.3 mile to a signed trail junction at the state park property line. Turn left here and begin a steeper climb on switchbacks up what appears to be an old fire line cut into the hillside. This is one of the portions of the trail given to you by those good volunteers mentioned previously.

After six switchbacks and a steep climb, the path gains the ridge at 2.1 miles and rejoins the old trail. Keep to the left and follow the ridge to a bench and junction at **2.3** miles with a trail that leads 0.1 mile to the first viewpoint overlooking the Spokane River. After taking in the view, walk back to the main trail and climb to a second viewpoint, **2.6** miles from the trailhead. This vista is studded with gnarly basalt outcrops that give the trail its Knothead name, the high point of the hike at 2,482 feet. Look downriver to Long Lake, now called Lake Spokane, and upriver to Nine Mile Falls and the confluence of the Little and big Spokane Rivers.

Admire the view, catch your breath, and follow the ridge crest as it begins dropping to the south to a junction with an old trail at

3.0 miles. Stay left and continue to drop steeply to a second trail junction at **3.4** miles; stay right here and walk through a section of the 2015 fire damage, switching back steeply for 0.3 mile to rejoin an old route and turn left at a gate marking private property.

At **3.8** miles, cross the upper portion of North River Park Lane and begin a long descent to the alternate Indian Painted Rocks Trailhead at State Route 291 and North River Park Lane. Cross North River Park Lane and turn east along the Little Spokane River, **4.8** miles from the trailhead. This is the Indian Painted Rocks trail (Hike 18).

Going Farther
The best way to get more exercise on this hike is to return to the trailhead and take the Little Spokane Upstream trail (Hike 20), which would add up to 5.8 miles round-trip to your hike. ■

20. Little Spokane Upstream

RATING	DISTANCE	HIKING TIME
★★★ ☆☆	**5.8 miles round-trip**	**3.5 hours**
ELEVATION GAIN	HIGH POINT	DIFFICULTY
540 feet	**2,040 feet**	◆◆◆◇

BEST MONTHS
Jan Feb Mar **Apr May Jun** Jul Aug **Sep Oct** Nov Dec

The Hike
Begin with a gentle walk along the Little Spokane River and climb through a rocky canyon to a much steeper trail ending with a splendid river view and forested hills.

Getting There
Take exit 280 from Interstate 90 in Spokane and follow Walnut Street north across the Maple Street Bridge to Francis Avenue. Turn left on Francis, drive west to Indian Trail Road, and turn right. Head north on Indian Trail Road for 4.7 miles to Rutter Parkway and continue straight,

following sharp downhill curves to a bridge crossing the Little Spokane River. Turn left into the parking area just past the bridge, where you'll find a restroom. The trailhead, 1,590 feet above sea level, is back across the bridge on the left side of the road.

PERMITS/CONTACT
Discover Pass required/Riverside State Park, (509) 465-5064,
www.parks.wa.gov

MAPS
USGS Dartford; state park map

TRAIL NOTES
Bikes and pets prohibited in the Little Spokane Natural Area;
expect mosquitoes in summer

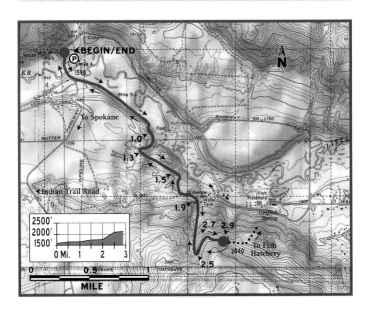

The Little Spokane River

The Trail

The first mile of this hike is a flat, pleasant walk that skirts a green river meadow to the north. It's an ideal trek for families with young children, where you'll likely get a glimpse of deer, wild turkeys, herons, or even moose. From the parking area, cross the Rutter Parkway bridge over the Little Spokane River and just beyond, turn east upriver. The trail drops gently to the meadow and heads upstream through tall grass along the southern edge of the meadow.

At **1.0** mile, the trail turns uphill to the south, dropping and then climbing on a moderate grade up a narrow, rocky defile to a forested bench where a seasonal wetland lies off to the right. This area, **1.3** miles from the trailhead, might be a good turnaround spot for families with young children. Beyond, the route turns through a narrow ravine where granite cliffs overshadow the pines.

Emerge from the ravine along a path pocked with what looks like micro volcano craters in the fine sand on the trail. These tiny dimples, around a half-inch in diameter, are traps set by those voracious insects, ant lions—sometimes called doodlebugs. Ants wander into the traps and can't climb the sand walls. The commotion alerts the ant lion, waiting just underground, which reaches up with jaws larger than the rest of its body and drags the ant underground for dinner. If you've never seen an ant lion and wouldn't wish such a gory end even to an ant, you can knock a few grains of sand into the pit of death with a pine needle and see the devil bug thrashing around, trying to find its meal. I have always wondered why there hasn't been a sci-fi movie about irradiated ant lions who grow to giant proportions and dig traps for humans.

Next, walk to a trail junction at **1.5** miles and stay right, climbing in 0.4 mile to the Riverside State Park boundary. Just beyond, a twin-track trail leads to the south up a canyon and the route becomes extremely steep for a half-mile. At **2.5** miles, the way leads left on a gentler traverse to a bench overlooking the Little Spokane River, **2.7** miles from the trailhead. Continue to your turnaround point at **2.9** miles, where the route begins to drop steeply toward the river.

You can return to the trailhead via the same route or follow a trail to the left as you reenter the state park. This path follows the southern and western boundary of the park, rejoining your route at the trail junction 1.5 miles from the trailhead.

Going Farther

You can continue from your turnaround point for another 1.2 miles to a fish hatchery and Griffith Spring, just east of St. George's School. The hatchery neighbors a second trailhead on the Little Spokane, popular with paddlers seeking a longer downstream ride to the confluence with the Spokane River. ■

21. Spokane House

RATING	DISTANCE	HIKING TIME
★★☆☆☆	3.3 miles round-trip	2 hours

ELEVATION GAIN	HIGH POINT	DIFFICULTY
40 feet	1,540 feet	◆◇◇◇◇

BEST MONTHS											
Jan	Feb	Mar	Apr	**May**	**Jun**	**Jul**	**Aug**	**Sep**	Oct	Nov	Dec

The Hike

Here's a family-friendly walk around a historic trading post along the rolling Spokane River.

Getting There

Take exit 280 from Interstate 90 in Spokane and follow Walnut Street north across the Maple Street Bridge to Francis Avenue. Turn left on Francis and follow it as it drops down and turns northwest, renamed Nine Mile Road and State Route 291. Follow it to the community of Nine Mile Falls and continue past the Nine Mile Falls Dam to the Spokane House parking area on the left. This is your trailhead, 1,540 feet above sea level.

The Trail

An excellent trek for families with young children, this gravel road-and-trail walk leads to the site of the Spokane House, an early trading post where Native Americans lived for centuries at the confluence of the Spokane and Little Spokane rivers. Before dams on the Columbia and Spokane Rivers were constructed, salmon

The trail at the Spokane House

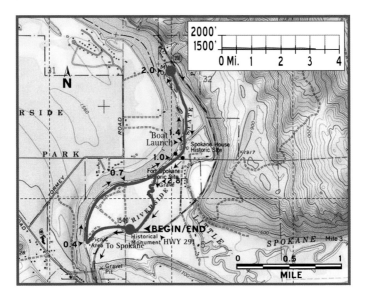

and steelhead navigated here and beyond. The fish were a primary source of food for Native American tribes, including the Spokanes, and abundant game made the area prime living space.

Interpretive signs along the route explain the history of the area and describe through journals written two centuries ago about life in the Inland Northwest. Start your journey by walking 0.4 mile along a path to the southwest, roughly paralleling SR 291 through a wooded forest where pink grass widows pop up in the spring. As the highway begins to climb to the Nine Mile Falls Dam, you'll approach the rapids of the Spokane River and look upstream to the dam. Turn downstream here on a twin-track road and walk along the river.

At **0.7** mile, you'll cross the main road leading to the site of the Spokane House. Continue walking downriver, passing an interpretive sign explaining the importance of salmon and steelhead to native tribes. At **1.0** mile, you'll see a gate and trail cutting across an open field to a paved road leading to a boat launch on Lake Spokane. When you reach the road, 1.4 miles from the trailhead,

PERMITS/CONTACT
Discover Pass required/Riverside State Park, (509) 465-5064,
www.parks.wa.gov

MAPS
USGS Nine Mile Falls; state park map

TRAIL NOTES
Bikes and pets prohibited in the Little Spokane Natural Area;
last mile of trail can be soggy in spring and early summer

turn left and follow it to the boat launch. Cross the paved boat trail parking area, where you'll find a restroom, to a trail leading north across a grassy meadow. This part of the path is designated as a section of the Washington State Palouse to Pines Loop birding trail.

The route now follows a narrow peninsula between the Spokane River—Lake Spokane to the west—and the Little Spokane River to the east, weaving through tangled brush to the confluence at **2.0** miles. This is a popular fishing spot, although steelhead and salmon are no longer caught here. Instead, giant suckers and largemouth bass are targeted by anglers who congregate here most of the year.

Since you can't continue without swimming from this point, turn around and follow your path back the way you came. At **2.8** miles, turn left and pass the site of the Spokane House with its interpretive signs. Follow the main gravel road south to the path leading right to the trailhead to finish this 3.3-mile hike.

Going Farther

You can extend this hike by 0.7 mile by returning the way you came. Another possibility for a longer trek would be to continue south on the boat launch road to its intersection with SR 291. Turn left and follow the shoulder of the highway to a bridge crossing the Little Spokane River and, on the other side, find a parking area and alternate trailhead for the Indian Painted Rocks (Hike 18) and Knothead Loop (Hike 19) trails. This could add up to 7 miles to your hike. ■

22. Milepost Zero

RATING	DISTANCE	HIKING TIME
★★★ ☆ ☆	5.8 miles round-trip	3 hours
ELEVATION GAIN	HIGH POINT	DIFFICULTY
710 feet	1,715 feet	◆ ◆ ◇ ◇ ◇

BEST MONTHS
Jan Feb **Mar Apr May Jun Jul Aug Sep Oct Nov** Dec

The Hike

This great family walk has everything the youngsters and parents will love, including a riverfront picnic spot and great views.

Getting There

Take exit 280 from Interstate 90 in Spokane and follow Walnut Street north across the Maple Street Bridge to Francis Avenue. Turn left on Francis and follow it as it drops down and turns northwest, renamed Nine Mile Road and State Route 291. Follow it to the community of Nine Mile Falls and turn left across Nine Mile Falls Dam. Pass the state park headquarters on the left (where you can purchase maps and get trail information) and drive to Sontag Park on the right for your parking area and the trailhead with a restroom. This was Milepost 0 of the 37-mile-long Centennial Trail. Because this park, 1,620 feet above sea level, is located just outside Riverside State Park, there is no Discover Pass requirement.

PERMITS/CONTACT
None required/Riverside State Park, (509) 465-5064, www.parks.wa.gov

MAPS
USGS Nine Mile Falls; state park map

TRAIL NOTES
Bikes and leashed dogs welcome; beware fast road bikes on the Centennial Trail portion

Hikers in wheelchairs are invited to park at the Carlson Road Trailhead, described in the Pine Bluff Loop trail (Hike 23); a Discover Pass is required there.

The Trail

The funny thing is, this hike no longer begins at Milepost 0, because the Centennial Trail was extended in 2016 for 2 miles west to the Nine Mile Recreation Area. Still, it's patrician hiking at its best, paved almost all the way with grades that can be navigated by those in wheelchairs with some assistance. You'll follow the paved route as it follows the Spokane River upstream, crossing Deep Creek Canyon and its picnic area before

The Spokane River

climbing to a bluff overlooking the river. Hike here in any season, but expect to wade through some snow in the winter. Spring is golden along the balsamroot-crowded bluff, and fall colors reflect in the quiet waters of the Nine Mile Reservoir.

Begin by walking a short distance southeast from Sontag Park to a well-marked crosswalk at Carlson Road. Follow the marked lane along Carlson to a new trailhead above the river, cross the road, and head into the pine woods where the trail climbs a hill and turns south to the Carlson Road Trailhead with its restroom, **0.6** mile from Sontag Park.

The Centennial Trail is gated just across the road from the trailhead. From this point, hikers should be aware of fast-traveling bicyclists, who should always let you know they're passing on the left. The route drops on a moderately steep grade, following the

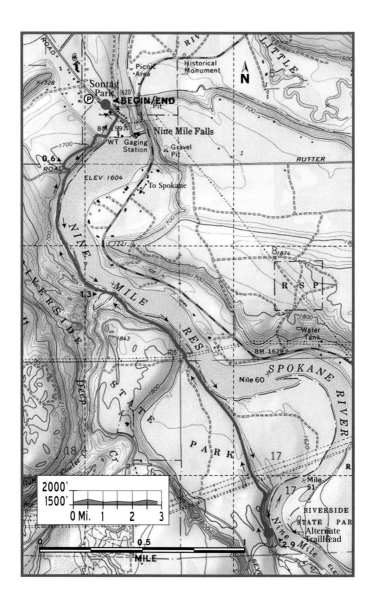

The bridge at Deep Creek on the Centennial Trail

curve of the Spokane River below on the left. If you choose, shoulders here are often wide enough to walk off the pavement. You'll pass an old Civilian Conservation Corps building and trailhead in about 0.3 mile, climb over a forested hump, and descend to a bridge crossing Deep Creek Canyon at the mouth of Coulee Creek, **1.3** miles from the trailhead.

This makes a great turnaround point for families with young children, with its picnic area and sandy lagoon at the mouth of the creek. You can explore the canyon along a sandy way trail, sometimes flooded in the spring, that weaves its way through basalt outcrops for almost 2 miles up the canyon, but most hikers opt for continuing along the Centennial Trail.

Beyond the bridge, the way climbs a moderately steep half-mile hill to a junction with the gravel State Park Road on the right. Round a corner to the south and climb to a wide bluff carpeted in the spring by yellow arrowleaf balsamroot and purple lupine. The route levels off here where the river turns east, away from the trail in a big elbow. You'll pass a couple of twin-track trails popular with mountain bikers and a restroom before arriving at the Seven Mile Trailhead with its restroom, **2.9** miles from the trailhead. Benches overlook the river below, a good spot to soak in the sunshine and the view. ∎

23. Pine Bluff Loop

RATING	DISTANCE	HIKING TIME
★★★★ ☆	6.6 miles round-trip	4.5 hours

ELEVATION GAIN	HIGH POINT	DIFFICULTY
740 feet	2,160 feet	◆◆◆◇

BEST MONTHS											
Jan	Feb	Mar	Apr	May	Jun	Jul	Aug	Sep	Oct	Nov	Dec

The Hike

The views up and down the Spokane River are well worth the extra sweat you'll generate climbing to this flower-filled bluff in Riverside State Park.

Getting There

Take exit 280 from Interstate 90 in Spokane and follow Walnut Street north across the Maple Street Bridge to Francis Avenue. Turn left on Francis and follow it as it drops down and turns northwest, renamed Nine Mile Road and State Route 291. Follow it to the community of Nine Mile Falls and turn left across Nine Mile Falls Dam. Turn left at the T intersection, Carlson Road, passing the state park headquarters (where you can purchase maps and get trail information). Continue south on Carlson as it climbs above the river and turns west. You'll find the parking area and restroom on the right, 1,750 feet above sea level. The trailhead is south, across Carlson Road, and west of the gated Centennial Trail.

PERMITS/CONTACT
Discover Pass required/Riverside State Park, (509) 465-5064, www.parks.wa.gov

MAPS
USGS Nine Mile Falls; state park map

TRAIL NOTES
Bikes and leashed dogs welcome; beware fast road bikes on the Centennial Trail portion

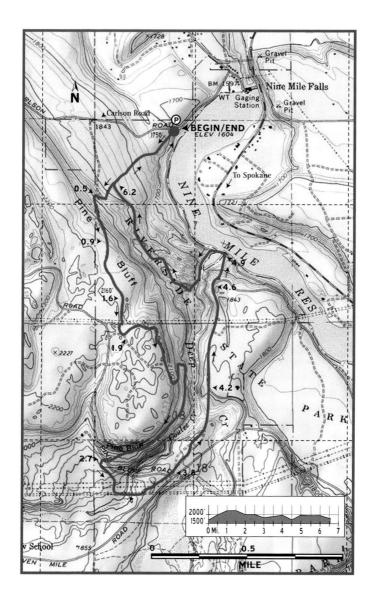

The Trail

If there's a single downside to hiking in Riverside State Park—or many of the hikes nearest rural Spokane—it's too many marked trails. Don't let the possibility of confusion stop you from hiking here, because the price you pay is small; taking a different trail will almost always get you where you want to go and back as long as you keep your sense of direction. Trails in the state park are also numbered to limit the confusion, but some connecting trails loop back to the main trail at a second junction.

Begin by hiking on a wide, well-used path on a gentle grade to the southwest in a pine forest. The trail grows a bit steeper and passes the first trail junction at **0.2** mile. Stay right and continue climbing to a second junction at **0.4** mile. Bypass this junction to the right and continue to a third junction at **0.5** mile, where you'll bear left on Trail 25 (so numbered because it is the main trail in Riverside State Park and 25 miles long). Continue climbing for 0.1 mile to yet another junction and stay right on Trail 25.

At **0.9** mile, the trail reaches the crest of Pine Bluff and turns left along an abandoned road. The meadow here is filled with golden arrowleaf balsamroot in the spring, the most ubiquitous wildflower throughout the Inland Northwest whose arrow-shaped leaves are soft and make excellent toilet paper in case you've forgotten the eleventh essential. (Please don't ask me how I know this.)

The route continues up and down along the edge of the bluff, serving terrific views both up and down the Nine Mile Reservoir portion of the Spokane River. Trail 25 leaves the abandoned road to the left at **1.2** miles and you'll follow the path past several minor trails, staying on Trail 25 to a bench and viewpoint at **1.6** miles. A second bench overlooks the river in another 0.1 mile while the trail passes on the right.

Find a fork in the trail at **1.9** miles and turn left on Trail 25, which begins dropping off the bluff and traverses the edge of basalt cliffs marking the northern face of Deep Creek Canyon. Switchback a couple of times and continue descending to a secondary, small trailhead on Pine Bluff Road at **2.7** miles.

Arrowleaf balsamroot along the Pine Bluff Loop trail

To continue, cross the road to the south and follow the trail as it descends a wide field underneath power lines before turning and recrossing the Pine Bluff Road just north of its intersection with Seven Mile Road, where the main Pine Bluff trailhead and restroom can be found at **3.8** miles. Walk north to a trail leading down along the wide upper end of Deep Creek Canyon, keeping to the right and climbing to the gated State Park Road and Deep Creek trailhead at **4.2** miles. Walk the road for 0.4 mile to the Deep Creek Overlook at **4.6** miles. This promontory looks at least 150 feet down upon the sandy bottom of the canyon, where you might imagine a stream named Deep Creek flows. Instead, the seasonal creek is named Coulee Creek.

Once you've exhausted the pixels on your smartphone, return to the road and turn left. About 100 feet down the road, look left for a pathway dropping steeply into the woods, follow it down to the paved Centennial Trail, and turn left across the bridge, **4.9** miles from the trailhead. (Don't worry if you miss this junction. Stay on the road and follow it to its junction with the Centennial Trail, about 0.3 mile, and turn left.)

Just across the bridge, turn left on the Deep Creek Interpretive Trail 411 and begin a half-mile climb through gnarly basalt formations. On the way up, note the rock causeway spanning a narrow gap in the trail, probably built by Civilian Conservation Corps workers. You may also see a rock climber's bolt placed in a cliff about halfway up the trail. At **5.5** miles, turn north on Trail 25/411 and hike another half-mile to a junction with Trail 400, **6.0** miles from the trailhead. Stay left on Trail 25 and then right on Trail 25 at the next junction, less than 0.1 mile beyond. At **6.2** miles, close the loop at the junction of Trails 25 and 402 and turn right toward the trailhead.

Going Farther

The easiest way to add miles to this hike would be to follow the Centennial Trail as far south as you want (it ends at the Washington-Idaho border, about 33 miles east). Keep in mind that you've got to return the way you came. ■

24. Dishman Hills Loop

RATING	DISTANCE	HIKING TIME
★★★☆☆	4.8 miles round-trip	2.5 hours
ELEVATION GAIN	**HIGH POINT**	**DIFFICULTY**
720 feet	2,420 feet	◆◆◆◇◇
BEST MONTHS		
Jan Feb Mar Apr May Jun Jul Aug Sep Oct Nov Dec		

The Hike

This prime piece of nature is the result of greater Spokane area residents who worked to protect the Dishman Hills Conservation Area, a delightful walk minutes from the center of the city.

Getting There

Follow Interstate 90 east to exit 285 for Sprague Avenue, and continue east past Thierman Road on Appleway Boulevard to Sargent Road and the entrance to Camp Caro on the right. Parking and the trailhead are in the big lot on the right, 2,100 feet above sea level. Restrooms are located in the Camp Caro lodge.

A Spokane Transit Authority bus route passes Camp Caro on Appleway Boulevard. Call (509) 328-RIDE or visit SpokaneTransit.com.

The Trail

There were a whole lot fewer trails in the Dishman Hills in 1953, when George Libby led his bunch of kids on hikes from Camp Caro into what seemed then like remote wilderness. In fact, it was a lot wilder in those days, but—thanks to the Dishman Hills Conservancy—it hasn't lost any of its beauty.

This is one hike where we were delighted to have a GPS-enabled iPad along to trace our route because we could only guess which signed trail to take among the many zigzags and crisscrosses. You're not likely to get lost, however, even if you have difficulty following the directions here. Simply follow the trails south for about 2 miles, then turn around and follow different trails north to the trailhead. When in doubt, listen for loudspeaker pages from auto sales lots to the north across Appleway Boulevard and follow the noise to the trailhead.

Begin by walking through a covered causeway in the 100-year-old Caro Lodge to a trail heading south in pine forest underneath Caro Cliff and a bench, keeping left at all trail junctions. At **0.8** mile, you pass a trail junction leading to an alternate trailhead on Siesta Drive. Turn right and cross a footbridge around Goldback Spring, on the right. Climb a wide gully to the southwest, then turn left downhill to a second alternate trailhead on 16th Avenue.

Just short of that trailhead, turn right and walk uphill along the natural area boundary, passing a water storage tank on the left. Beyond, **1.8** miles from the trailhead, you'll pass a junction with a trail leading to Eagle Peak. Stay left here and continue climbing into a section of

PERMITS/CONTACT
None required/Spokane County Parks and Recreation,
(509) 477-4730, www.spokanecounty.org/parks

MAPS
USGS Spokane NE; county map

TRAIL NOTES
Leashed dogs OK

Crossing a bridge near Goldback Spring

the forest that was destroyed by wildfire in 2008. You'll see a number of luxurious homes perched on the ridge to the south, some within feet of the fire's damage. The trail climbs over a broad, fire-scarred ridge, turns west, and begins looping back to the south, **2.2** miles from the trailhead.

Stay right at an unsigned trail junction in another 0.1 mile, and at **2.4** miles, find a signed trail leading right to Eagle Peak, the high point of your hike at 2,420 feet. After taking in a view from Eagle Peak that includes the Spokane Valley and Mount Spokane to the north, return the way you came and turn right at the Eagle Peak junction.

Walk south about 0.1 mile to the Ridge Top Trail and turn right downhill, staying left at the next two trail junctions. The trail now descends on a series of granite slabs to the southwest to a bench and trail junction leading to the left to a trailhead at Edgehill Park,

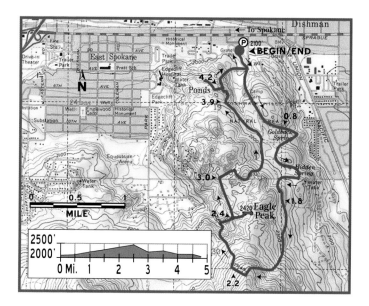

3.9 miles from the trailhead. Follow it about 100 feet to a path turning right to East and West Ponds and continue downhill to the junction with the ponds trail, **4.2** miles from the trailhead.

Turn left for a view of the ponds, then return to the junction and continue down a series of steep steps to the broad lawn of Camp Caro and the trailhead.

Going Farther

You can extend your hike by about 1.8 miles by following the Deep Ravine Trail to the east from Camp Caro, then taking trails past Siesta Drive and 16th Avenue trailheads along the natural area boundary. ■

25. Big Rock Loop

RATING	DISTANCE	HIKING TIME
★★★★☆	**4.9 miles round-trip**	**3.5 hours**

ELEVATION GAIN	HIGH POINT	DIFFICULTY
1,150 feet	**3,550 feet**	◆◆◆◆◇

BEST MONTHS
Jan Feb Mar **Apr May Jun Jul Aug Sep Oct** Nov Dec

The Hike

This prime suburban adventure leads to a popular rockclimbing area along open slopes and shady forest glades less than a dozen miles from downtown Spokane.

Getting There

Take Interstate 90 east to exit 287 and follow Argonne Road south past Sprague Avenue to Dishman-Mica Road. Follow Dishman-Mica 2.4 miles to Schafer Road, turn right on Schafer, and follow it to 44th Avenue. Turn right on 44th, drive one block to Woodruff Road, and turn left. Drive to Holman Road and turn right, following Holman to the Iller Creek Trailhead parking area, 2,400 feet above sea level. A private road leads uphill to the left. The parking area is often crowded; make sure you don't block the private drive. There's a restroom at the trailhead.

Big Rock is actually pretty big

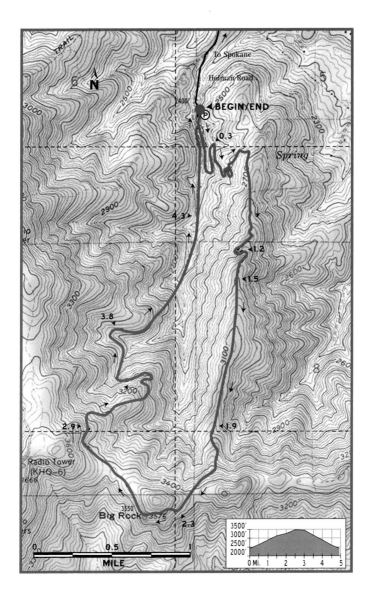

To Spokane

Holman Road

ⓟ ◄BEGIN/END

◄0.3

Spring

◄1.2

◄1.5

4.3►

3.8▼

2.9►

◄1.9

Radio Tower
(KHQ-6)
2666

Big Rock *3576*

3550

◄2.3

N

TRAIL

| 0 | 0.5 | 1 |
MILE

3500'					
3000'					
2500'					
2000'					
0 Mi.	1	2	3	4	5

The view of Palouse country

A Spokane Transit Authority bus route passes within a mile of this trailhead. Call (509) 328-RIDE or visit SpokaneTransit.com.

The Trail

Though it doesn't climb to alpine wilderness, the loop hike around Big Rock and the Rocks of Sharon feels like you're walking in wild country. That may have something to do with the fact that this forest gem is the Iller Creek unit of the Dishman Hills Conservation Area.

Start by walking uphill through a gate and turn left on the first trail. The path begins climbing from the get-go and doesn't let up for more than a mile. This section is best hiked early on a spring morning, when the brushy, open west-facing slopes might still provide some shade. The path climbs in eight switchbacks, passing a way trail **0.3** mile from the trailhead. In another half-mile, you'll reach the crest of the ridge and views open in three directions. That's Mica Peak to the east, decorated with a radar dome. The trail here glistens in morning sun with particles of mica in the rocks and gravel.

At **1.2** miles, sparse pines begin to provide more shade as you climb along the ridge and the route dips gently into a saddle forested with pines and fir, **1.5** miles from the trailhead. Keep left at a junction here and climb to a second junction at **1.9** miles. Stay left again and continue as the trail begins climbing more steeply. At **2.1** miles, look down in the brush where an old Ford pickup truck expired and in another tenth of a mile, arrive at a trail junction. Stay right on the Stevens Creek Trail and at **2.3** miles, reach a junction with a side route leading to a viewpoint of the Rocks of Sharon. Turn right for the view, then return to the junction and turn left on the Stevens Creek Trail.

The route traverses to the west toward that big rock jutting out of the hillside. Pass a trail leading downhill to an alternate trailhead on the Stevens Creek Road and continue walking toward that big rock named—spoiler alert—Big Rock. The trail passes this 3,576-foot-high chunk of granite to the north, then turns downhill along a ridge to the east, where you can look west to several radio and television towers on a hill named—another big surprise—Tower Mountain, a.k.a. Krell Hill.

Past Big Rock, the trail descends to a saddle with views to the south of the Palouse farmland and Steptoe Butte, staying left at the western junction with the viewpoint trail. At **2.9** miles, stay right with a way trail leading toward Tower Mountain and enter an evergreen forest. The route then turns downhill to the north, following the crest of a minor ridge to a junction with a trail crossing Iller Creek to your right. Stay left, switchback, and cross a spring at **3.8** miles. The trail drops into a soggy draw and follows Iller Creek downstream to what might be a wet crossing in spring, **4.3** miles from the trailhead. Continue above the creek to the trailhead. ∎

26. Beacon Hill

RATING	DISTANCE	HIKING TIME
★☆☆☆☆	3.8 miles round-trip	2 hours

ELEVATION GAIN	HIGH POINT	DIFFICULTY
610 feet	2,600 feet	◆◆◇◇◇

BEST MONTHS
Jan Feb Mar **Apr May** Jun Jul Aug **Sep Oct** Nov Dec

The Hike

Watch airplanes landing below you on this climb to views of the Spokane River and Valley, popular with lunchtime bicyclists, hikers, and trail runners.

Getting There

Follow Interstate 90 east to exit 283B and exit onto 3rd Avenue, driving east to Freya Street. Turn left on Freya, which becomes Freya Way and later Greene Street, crossing the Spokane River. After climbing around a turn to the left, Greene turns into Market Street and intersects Euclid Avenue at a stoplight. Turn right (east) on Euclid, which turns into Frederick Avenue, and continue east on Frederick to Havana Street. Turn left on Havana and drive uphill two blocks to a parking area and trailhead just east above Minnehaha Park, 2,020 feet above sea level. Restrooms are located in Minnehaha Park.

A Spokane Transit Authority bus route loops past the southwest corner of Minnehaha Park. Call (509) 328-RIDE or visit SpokaneTransit.com.

PERMITS/CONTACT
None required/Spokane Parks and Recreation,
(509) 625-6200, www.spokaneparks.org

MAPS
USGS Spokane NE

TRAIL NOTES
Leashed dogs OK; bikes welcome

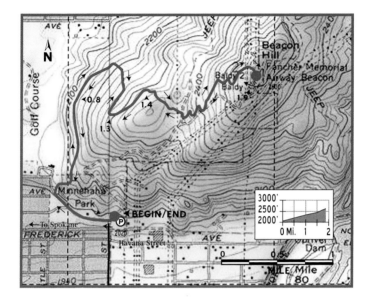

The Trail

This hike is so close to the city but a long way from civilization. We took this trail in early June and saw a doe and two fawns, spotted eagles and ravens soaring above, and shared a summit picnic with a couple of friendly marmots. Expect to see a few mountain bikes on this hike as well, although the route described here avoids many of the steeper trails preferred by hardcore daredevils.

Begin by dropping down into Minnehaha Park and following the paved trail past restrooms and big rock posts near the northwest end of the park. Turn right off the trail on a wide gravel path, climbing north and passing above the parking lot of the Esmeralda Golf Course. Reach a fork in the trail at **0.8** mile and stay left, traversing a forest along a west-facing hillside.

The trail turns in a wide switchback to the north and begins climbing more steeply to reach a viewpoint at **1.3** miles of the old railroad facility and Hillyard community.

Beacon Hill is popular with mountain bikers as well as hikers

In another 0.1 mile, reach a second junction with a double track trail swooping downhill, and stay on the single track leading north. The trail now turns east and climbs to a saddle before dropping into a swale and crossing under power lines. From here, stay on the single-track trail as it climbs in about twelve switchbacks up the open slopes of Beacon Hill—the USGS survey marker on the summit identifies the hill as Baldy—to the towers on the summit and, this should come as no surprise, a beacon. The best viewpoint of the river and Felts Field airport is on the steeper south side of the hill, **1.9** miles from the trailhead.

Going Farther

Several trails and old jeep tracks circle Beacon Hill and lead down to Shields Park, about a mile east of your trailhead. Shields is a popular rock-climbing area, with steeper pathways up Beacon Hill. ■

27. Saltese Conservation Area

RATING	DISTANCE	HIKING TIME
★★ ☆☆☆	5.0 miles round-trip	3 hours

ELEVATION GAIN	HIGH POINT	DIFFICULTY
760 feet	2,630 feet	◆◆◆ ◇◇

BEST MONTHS
Jan Feb Mar Apr **May Jun Jul Aug Sep** Oct Nov Dec

The Hike
Expect company on this pleasant walk in the foothills above Liberty Lake, where cyclists and joggers from nearby tech companies work out during their lunch breaks.

Getting There
Drive east on Interstate 90 to exit 293 for Barker Road. Turn right on Barker and drive a half-mile to Sprague Avenue. Turn left on Sprague and drive almost a mile to Henry Road, then turn right, driving 0.8 mile to the trailhead and parking area on the left, 2,080 feet above sea level. You'll find a restroom at the trailhead.

The Trail
This excellent piece of hiking and biking is brought to you courtesy of the Spokane County Conservation Futures program. Since 2011, the county and volunteers from groups like the Washington Trails Association have developed this naturally tree-free land—called a

PERMITS/CONTACT
None required/Spokane County Parks and Recreation, (509) 477-4730, www.spokanecounty.org/parks

MAPS
USGS Greenacres, USGS Liberty Lake; county map

TRAIL NOTES
Leashed dogs OK; bikes and equestrians welcome

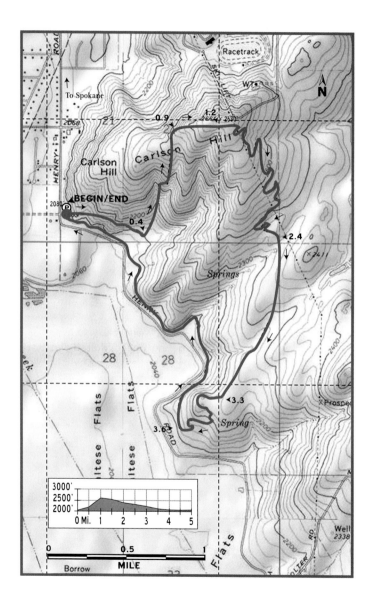

Liberty Lake from the Saltese Uplands Trail

shrub steppe—into a nearby haven for cityfolk looking to get a little outdoor exercise.

The openness of the rock-strewn hills makes spotting wildlife easy, and you're likely to see deer and coyotes in the canyons or the greener sections of the trail. Bobcats and badgers have been reported here, but the only badgering I encountered was B. B. Hardbody telling me to keep up with her. I answered by mumbling something I hoped she didn't hear.

The pathway leads briefly uphill along a south-facing hillside before dropping into a wide meadow, **0.4** mile from the trailhead. Here a number of trails fan out, generally heading to the east and south. Turn left at this junction on a single-track trail that climbs steeply toward the north around rocky outcrops and follows a fence line climbing to a viewpoint of the Spokane Valley and I-90 below, **0.9** mile from the trailhead.

The route continues to climb at a fairly vigorous angle to a hilltop viewpoint along the fenceline at **1.2** miles. In another 0.1 mile, you'll begin a series of about sixteen switchbacks that roughly follow a power line you cross under at the top and bottom of the hill. Views here are down to posh houses that ring Liberty Lake. At the bottom, the trail crosses a service road along the power line and at **2.3** miles, reach a junction with the Uplands Loop and Summit Loop Trails.

Keep left and follow the Uplands Loop Trail, staying left at a junction with the Short Draw Trail, **2.4** miles from the trailhead. The way now climbs to a ridge overlooking Henry Road at **3.3** miles, then drops in steep switchbacks down the crest of a ridge to a junction with the Uplands Loop Trail at **3.6** miles. Beyond, the trail heads down to parallel Henry Road, ducks through a welcome grove of trees, and climbs around to the parking area at **5.0** miles.

Going Farther

More than 7 miles of trails can be hiked throughout the Saltese Uplands. Trails are well marked, providing a choice of loop or out-and-back hikes that can be combined or retraced for longer treks. ∎

28. Antoine Peak

RATING	DISTANCE	HIKING TIME
★★★☆	**5.7 miles round-trip**	**3.5 hours**
ELEVATION GAIN	**HIGH POINT**	**DIFFICULTY**
1,270 feet	**3,373 feet**	◆◆◆◇◇
BEST MONTHS		
Jan Feb Mar Apr **May Jun Jul Aug Sep Oct** Nov Dec		

The Hike

Walk through a wild suburban forest to the summit of a prominent local mountain where critters roam the land and sky along a corridor that links the area with Mount Spokane.

Getting There

Drive east on Interstate 90 to exit 291B and turn left on Sullivan Road. Drive north for 2.2 miles on Sullivan to Wellesley Avenue and turn left. Follow Wellesley to Progress Street and turn right. Drive to a T intersection with Forker Road and turn right, following Forker

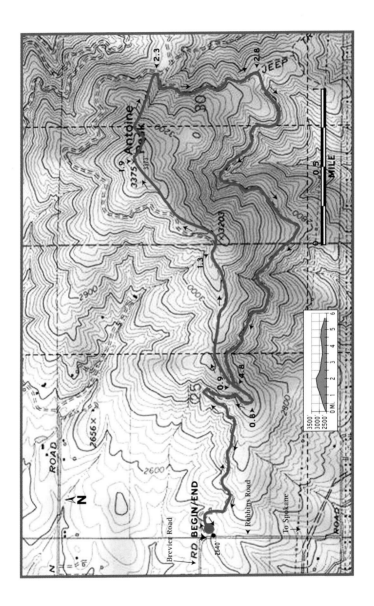

0.4 mile to Jacobs Road, where you'll turn right and drive 0.7 mile to Robbins Road. Turn left on Robbins and follow it to the trailhead in 0.4 mile, 2,640 feet above sea level. Be aware: we found broken auto glass in the parking area.

The Trail

Here's another of the emerald gems acquired by the Spokane County Conservation Futures program, 1,076 acres of hills and pine forests filled with wildlife. Expect to see deer and perhaps elk and watch the skies above—this is part of the Palouse to Pines Loop birding trail—for hawks, eagles, and ravens. The trail is popular both in summer for hiking and biking and winter for cross-country skiing and snowshoeing.

Begin by climbing along a road into thick forest, or a single-track trail above the road to the right. The road and trail merge in **0.8** mile and the road is more pleasant hiking in shaded forest decorated with ocean spray in early summer. At **0.9** mile, stay left where the road forks and walk another 0.4 mile to a second fork, where you'll climb to the right. This is the route to the summit of Antoine Peak, which is **1.9** miles from the trailhead. You'll find a viewpoint on rocks past two radio towers on the right, where you can see the Spokane Valley and Rathdrum Prairie to the southeast. Look east to timber-covered slopes of the conservation area, where another trailhead is located.

After you've taken in the view, find the road that leads steeply down to the south, dropping 360 feet in less than a half-mile. There's a kinder, gentler road at the bottom, **2.3** miles from the trailhead. Turn right, following the road through open forest as it rounds several

The view from the Antoine Peak trail

gullies on a downhill traverse. After a half-mile, you'll find a junction with a second road heading downhill. Turn right here, **2.8** miles from the trailhead.

The old road now traverses into a wide gully, then drops around a ridge before climbing into a second gully and climbing out of it. Finally, it climbs toward the summit road junction, **4.8** miles from the trailhead. Turn left at the junction and follow it downhill to the trailhead at **5.7** miles.

Going Farther
The best way to make a longer hike is to turn around at the summit of Antoine Peak, retrace your steps on the summit road for 0.6 mile, and turn right on the road that circles Antoine Peak to the north. This road generally traverses around the peak and joins the route described above, 3.4 miles from the trailhead, making a round-trip hike of 6.8 miles. ■

29. Liberty Creek Loop

RATING	DISTANCE	HIKING TIME
★★★★☆	**8.4 miles round-trip**	**5 hours**

ELEVATION GAIN	HIGH POINT	DIFFICULTY
1,520 feet	**3,560 feet**	◆◆◆◆◇

BEST MONTHS
Jan Feb Mar Apr **May Jun Jul Aug Sep** Oct Nov Dec

The Hike

Cedar forests, baby waterfalls, and splashing creeks are the stars of this long climb above Liberty Lake.

Getting There

Drive east on Interstate 90 to exit 296 and turn right on Liberty Lake Road, following it to Sprague Avenue. Turn left on Sprague past the golf course and follow to the right, where it becomes Neyland Road. Follow Neyland past a Y intersection, keeping right, to Lakeside Road. Turn right on Lakeside and follow it to Zephyr Road. Turn right on Zephyr to the Liberty Lake Regional Park entrance, where you'll be asked to pay an entrance fee ($2 in 2017; free between Labor Day weekend and Memorial Day but the gate may be closed). Restrooms are located in the park. The trailhead is 2,100 feet above sea level.

The Trail

Liberty Lake Regional Park, with its campground, cabins, and picnic areas, is a wonderful low-budget getaway from urban Spokane. The lake is at its best in early summer, before persistent algae blooms cloud the water, but the trails leading up Liberty Creek attract hikers, mountain bikers, and equestrians most any time of the year.

The relative lack of territorial views might disappoint, but cooling shade provided by dense forest—including a marvelous grove of old cedars—might more than compensate on a hot summer day. If you've parked in the lower lot by the entrance booth, hike south along trails that traverse above the campground to the kiosk and gate marking

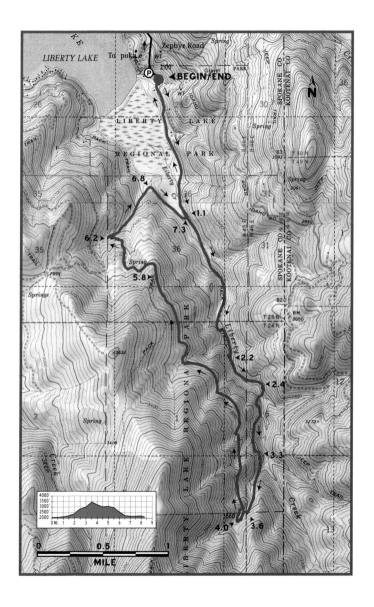

A photo op from "my" switchback on the Liberty Creek Trail

the Liberty Creek Trail. The route climbs very gently along the creek, passing a trail junction at **1.1** miles, your return route. Stay left and continue another quarter-mile to a bridge crossing the creek.

You'll recross the creek again at **2.2** miles, then enter the grove of splendid old cedars, a popular picnicking and turnaround spot for families with youngsters (or oldsters!) who might balk at the steeper climb ahead. Cross the creek here at **2.4** miles, and begin a series of steep switchbacks, climbing more than 300 feet in less than a quarter-mile. Even though I claim the final switchback as mine, in truth it was the crew of Washington Trails Association volunteers accompanying your malingering correspondent who did the actual work. The path at this turn affords the only view of Liberty Lake and Antoine Peak you'll get on this hike.

PERMITS/CONTACT
Parking pass required/Spokane County Parks and Recreation,
(509) 477-4730, www.spokanecounty.org/parks

MAPS
USGS Liberty Lake; county map

TRAIL NOTES
Leashed dogs OK; bikes welcome; equestrians on
Edith Hansen Riding Trail

From my switchback, the trail climbs more gently to the south, crossing branches of Liberty Creek before reaching a waterfall at **3.3** miles. The trail here switches back and climbs above the waterfall. It's steep and the pathway slants downhill, making tough going for a short quarter-mile. Once above the waterfall, the way eases and crosses the creek at **3.6** miles, then passes Hughes Cabin, **4.0** miles from the trailhead. The cabin and trail are named for R. W. Hughes, a Spokane County Parks staffer of more than thirty-one years who helped establish this trail.

Keep right at the cabin and follow the wide Edith Hansen Riding Trail downhill for nearly 2 miles to a junction with a trail heading left to Mica Peak, a popular mountain bike route, **5.8** miles from the trailhead. Stay right and continue downhill, keeping right at a second junction at **6.2** miles.

Now you'll drop more steeply down a forested gully to the wetlands at the south end of Liberty Lake, passing a gate at **6.8** miles and crossing a meadow and Liberty Creek to close the loop at **7.3** miles. Turn left and walk 1.1 miles to the trailhead.

Going Farther
You can add at least 4.5 round-trip miles to your hike by turning left at the Mica Peak trail junction. This route soon leaves the county park and climbs on a confusing jumble of old jeep roads to the 5,205-foot mountain, capped by a Federal Aviation Administration facility. ∎

MOUNT SPOKANE

30. Hay Ridge Loop

RATING	DISTANCE	HIKING TIME
★★★☆☆	5.0 miles round-trip	2.5 hours

ELEVATION GAIN	HIGH POINT	DIFFICULTY
220 feet	4,220 feet	◆◇◇◇◇

BEST MONTHS
Jan Feb Mar Apr May **Jun Jul Aug Sep Oct** Nov Dec

The Hike

Save this walk for a foggy or rainy day—if indeed there is such a thing in sunny Inland Northwest—because most views are of beautiful evergreens, subalpine wildflowers, and the occasional moose, deer, or black bear.

Getting There

Drive east on Interstate 90 to exit 287 and turn left onto Argonne Road. Follow Argonne, which joins Bruce Road, for about 8.5 miles to a roundabout at Mount Spokane Park Drive (State Route 206). Follow Mount Spokane Park Drive for about 13 miles to Mount Spokane State Park. The park is open from 6:30 a.m. to dusk. Drive about 2 miles to the wide parking area on the right, just before a sharp switchback on Mount Spokane Park Drive. This trailhead is located at 3,897 feet.

PERMITS/CONTACT
Discover Pass required/Mount Spokane State Park, (509) 238-4258, www.parks.wa.gov

MAPS
USGS Kit Carson; excellent PDF trail map from Friends of Mount Spokane State Park, www.mountspokane.org

TRAIL NOTES
Leashed dogs OK; bikes and equestrians welcome

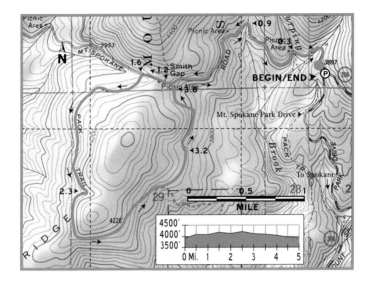

The Trail

The Lower Mount Kit Carson Loop Road, which serves as your trail, is extremely popular throughout the year and perhaps used most heavily in the winter as a snowshoe and cross-country ski venue. Portions are also open to snowmobilers.

In summer, the route is shaded for comfortable hiking on all but the hottest days, and wildflowers like western spring beauty and trillium bloom well into June. Find the trailhead across Mount Spokane Park Drive near its hairpin turn, and drop to the wide Lower Mount Kit Carson Loop Road, which passes a trail junction in **0.3** mile. Stay on the loop road, crossing several streams with nearby picnic tables in the next half-mile, then crossing a tributary to Burping Brook at **0.9** mile. (It may have belched silently but never really blasted one out like a soda-guzzling teenager.)

Next, begin a gentle descent to a junction with Trail 140/170 and note the junction on the left, **1.2** miles from the trailhead, your return path on this frying-pan loop. Continue another

0.1 mile to Smith Gap, where you'll find a vault toilet and a spiffy new warming hut constructed by Friends of Mount Spokane State Park with grant monies from the Johnston-Fix Foundation. The hut is decorated with imaginative clothing and equipment racks made from cross-country ski bindings, pole baskets, and carved wall hangings. After your visit, head west on the loop road for another 0.2

The warming hut

mile to a junction with Trail 170 on the left at **1.6** miles.

Turn left on 170 and climb along a green forested hillside on Hay Ridge, keeping to the right of a way trail leading to a high point on the ridge at **2.3** miles. Continue on Trail 170 as it curves widely around Hay Ridge, offering only tree-ka-boo views of the Spokane Valley to the south and west. You'll pass a couple of old logging roads that climb to Hay Ridge; stay on a descending traverse as you round the ridge and head north. At **3.2** miles, Trail 140 climbs up from the south to join your route, now designated 140/170.

Stay left as the path continues to drop gently past a couple of areas that can get damp in the spring, finally emerging onto the Lower Mount Kit Carson Loop Road and Smith Gap at **3.8** miles. Turn right for the 1.2-mile walk to the parking area.

Going Farther

Probably the best way to hike farther would be to continue up the Lower Mount Kit Carson Loop Road for a couple of miles, returning the way you came. This road climbs past a junction with Day Road and passes several picnic areas on its way to a circumnavigation of Day Mountain to the north. ■

31. Day Mountain–Mount Kit Carson Traverse

RATING	DISTANCE	HIKING TIME
★ ★ ★ ★ ☆	6.7 miles round-trip	3.5 hours

ELEVATION GAIN	HIGH POINT	DIFFICULTY
1,550 feet	5,282 feet	◆ ◆ ◆ ◇ ◇

BEST MONTHS
Jan Feb Mar Apr May **Jun Jul Aug Sep** Oct Nov Dec

The Hike

Climb through splendid old subalpine forest and bear grass gardens to the summits of two mountain neighbors of Mount Spokane.

Getting There

Drive east on Interstate 90 to exit 287 and turn left onto Argonne Road. Follow Argonne, which joins Bruce Road, for about 8.5 miles to a roundabout at Mount Spokane Park Drive (State Route 206). Follow Mount Spokane Park Drive for about 13 miles to Mount Spokane State Park. The park is open from 6:30 a.m. to dusk. Drive 3 miles to Summit Road, opposite a large paved parking area, and turn left. Follow Summit for 1 mile to the Bald Knob picnic area, campground, restrooms, and trailhead, 5,125 feet above sea level.

The Trail

Mount Spokane, 5,883 feet high, and the state park that surrounds it is an absolute treasure for hikers and mountain bikers in the summer and skiers and snowshoers in the winter. Trails in the summer are lined with wildflowers, wildlife abounds, vistas can't be beaten, and the alpine air is cooler than the valleys below, making uphill chugs more tolerable. All of this is less than 50 minutes from the city center.

This hike, like all trails but one on Mount Spokane, begins at Bald Knob, where you'll find one of the best deals for primitive camping at

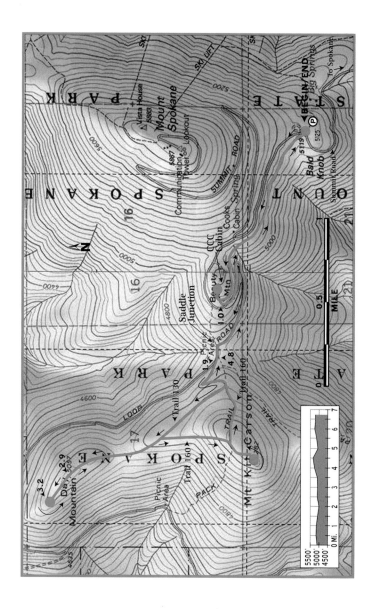

PERMITS/CONTACT
Discover Pass required/Mount Spokane State Park,
(509) 238-4258, www.parks.wa.gov

MAPS
USGS Kit Carson, USGS Mt. Spokane; excellent PDF trail map from
Friends of Mount Spokane State Park, www.mountspokane.org

TRAIL NOTES
Leashed dogs OK; bikes and equestrians welcome

any state park in Washington. Make it your headquarters for five days of alpland trekking.

Start by crossing the road and finding Trail 130, which traverses the hillside below Summit Road for a mile under firs and open forest where the bear grass in June is so thick it almost looks like the snow hasn't melted. You'll find a junction and a trail leading to a Civilian Conservation Corps cabin uphill to the right. Your route is downhill to the left, but before heading that way, climb up to look at the cabin, the rockwork surrounding it, and perhaps reflect on the handiwork of the CCC more than eight decades ago. The stove and firewood inside are the gifts of the Winter Knights Snowmobile Club.

Return to the trail junction, follow it down to the Upper Mount Kit Carson Loop Road, and turn left, hiking the wide double track downhill and switching back to Saddle Junction, **1.9** miles from the trailhead. Look to the left for Trail 130/160 and take it as it climbs and switches back to a fork with Trail 160. Stay right on Trail 130 as it traverses in alpine forest around Mount Kit Carson. Walk another half-mile to the junction with Trail 160 as it returns from the summit of Mount Kit Carson. You'll be taking this trail on your return.

For now, keep right on Trail 130 as it crosses a saddle and climbs the broad ridge crest to a wide alpine meadow on the summit of Day Mountain, 5,057 feet above sea level and **2.9** miles from the trailhead. The trail drops to a spectacular rocky viewpoint overlooking the Spokane Valley, your turnaround spot at **3.2** miles. To not picnic here is to suffer extreme regret and guilt for eternity.

Meadow grass along the trail to Day Mountain

When you are ready to return, walk back down to the saddle and junction with Trail 160 and turn right. This trail climbs gently, then very steeply, up to the summit of 5,282-foot Mount Kit Carson, crossing a junction with an old pack trail and Trail 160 as it returns from the summit. Continue climbing around a couple of switchbacks to the summit viewpoint. In the event you didn't picnic on Day Mountain, Lucifer himself will drag you screaming to hell if you don't feast here.

Finally, retrace your route to the old pack trail and turn right on Trail 160, traversing around Kit Carson and dropping steeply down to the first 130/160 fork above Saddle Junction, **4.8** miles from the trailhead. Stay right and return to Saddle Junction, retracing your steps back to the trailhead.

Going Farther

For a marathon adventure, stay on Trail 130 as it descends from Day Mountain and crosses the Upper Mount Kit Carson Loop Road, where it becomes the Round the Mountain Trail. Completing the entire circumnavigation of Mount Spokane and returning to Bald Knob would be a hike of at least 13 miles and more vertical than you can count. ■

32. Beauty Mountain Loop

RATING	DISTANCE	HIKING TIME
★★★★	5.8 miles round-trip	3.5 hours

ELEVATION GAIN	HIGH POINT	DIFFICULTY
2,200 feet	5,125 feet	♦♦♦♦

BEST MONTHS											
Jan	Feb	Mar	Apr	May	Jun	Jul	Aug	Sep	Oct	Nov	Dec

The Hike

Don't let the fact that you get expansive vistas on only portions of this climb deter you from enjoying this grand forest walk.

Getting There

Drive east on Interstate 90 to exit 287 and turn left onto Argonne Road. Follow Argonne, which joins Bruce Road, for about 8.5 miles to a roundabout at Mount Spokane Park Drive (State Route 206). Follow Mount Spokane Park Drive for about 13 miles to Mount Spokane State Park. The park is open from 6:30 a.m. to dusk. Drive 3 miles to Summit Road, opposite a large paved parking area, and turn left. Follow Summit for 1 mile to the Bald Knob picnic area, campground, restrooms, and trailhead, 5,125 feet above sea level.

The Trail

The Bald Knob Campground is an excellent and affordable base camp for exploring all the delightful trails around Mount Spokane State Park, arguably one of the best state parks in Washington. It attracts skiers, snowshoers, and snowmobilers in the winter and hikers, bicyclists, wildlife watchers, and equestrians in the summer. If you've time for only one hike on your visit to the Inland Northwest, make it one here.

The loop hike to Beauty Mountain begins with serious downhill travel and concludes with a long but gentler return. A clockwise direction is suggested for the loop, but if your knees suffer more on downhill than uphill stretches, hike this trail in reverse direction.

PERMITS/CONTACT
Discover Pass required/Mount Spokane State Park,
(509) 238-4258, www.parks.wa.gov

MAPS
USGS Kit Carson, USGS Mt. Spokane; excellent PDF trail map from
Friends of Mount Spokane State Park, www.mountspokane.org

TRAIL NOTES
Leashed dogs OK; bikes and equestrians welcome

Begin by walking downhill past the restrooms and Bald Knob picnic shelter on a well-defined path that descends an open ridge to the east. Find a trail junction at **0.3** mile and turn right, descending sharply to the southwest toward Summit Road. At **0.8** mile, just before striking the road, turn right on Trail 131 and drop steeply to the junction of Summit Road and Mount Spokane Park Drive. Cross Summit to the south and take Trail 100 leading to the west, traversing the forest below.

The path climbs into a gully and crosses Deadman Creek, **1.5** miles from Bald Knob, before dropping in huge chunks toward a deep gully that hosts a tributary to Burping Brook. We heard no burping as we plummeted more than 600 vertical feet, perhaps because our knees were screaming. At **2.4** miles, just before reaching a picnic area, pass Trail 103 and continue in switchbacks down to the picnic area at a hairpin turn just off Mount Spokane Park Drive. This is the lower end of your hike and a shady, cool spot for a rest.

From here, follow Trail 100 to the west and cross a creek on a footlog, then begin climbing a forested ridge above another belching tributary. At **2.9** miles, turn right on Trail 110 and continue upward in forest, arriving at a crossing of the main channel of Burping Brook at **3.5** miles. The trail continues to climb steadily in four switchbacks to Saddle Junction, **4.5** miles from Bald Knob.

From here, follow the Upper Mount Kit Carson Loop Road to the right as it climbs more gently around a switchback and passes a junction with Trail 130 at **5.1** miles. Climb to the right here, noting where

Burping Brook never excused itself

Trail 130 turns east to the Civilian Conservation Corps cabin and the top of 5,200-foot Beauty Mountain. This splendid cabin, with its stove and firewood furnished by the Winter Knights Snowmobile Club, was built in 1934 and rebuilt in 1998.

When you've finished admiring the craftwork, return to Trail 130 and head east, traversing open slopes with views of the Spokane Valley below and the summit of Mount Spokane above. The trail meanders through alpine forest decorated with bear grass blossoms in June and crosses a seep where you might see yellow monkeyflower, paintbrush, or shooting star throughout early summer. At **5.8** miles, cross Summit Road to Bald Knob.

Going Farther

The best way to extend this hike might be to follow Trails 130 and 160 to the left from Saddle Junction to the summit of Mount Kit Carson, returning the way you came. That would add about 1.5 miles round-trip to your hike. ■

33. Vista House

RATING	DISTANCE	HIKING TIME
★ ★ ★ ★ ★	5.9 miles round-trip	3.5 hours
ELEVATION GAIN	HIGH POINT	DIFFICULTY
680 feet	5,883 feet	◆ ◆ ◆ ◇ ◇

BEST MONTHS		
Jan Feb Mar Apr May **Jun Jul Aug Sep** Oct Nov Dec		

The Hike

Here is the ultimate alpine trek near Spokane, taking you across wildflower meadows into fir-forest wildlife havens to the summit of Mount Spokane and its historic Vista House.

Getting There

Drive east on Interstate 90 to exit 287 and turn left onto Argonne Road. Follow Argonne, which joins Bruce Road, for about 8.5 miles to a roundabout at Mount Spokane Park Drive (State Route 206). Follow Mount Spokane Park Drive for about 13 miles to Mount Spokane State Park. The park is open from 6:30 a.m. to dusk. Drive 3 miles to Summit Road, opposite a large paved parking area, and turn left. Follow Summit for 1 mile to the Bald Knob picnic area, campground, restrooms, and trailhead, 5,125 feet above sea level.

The Trail

Several trailhead options offering both shorter and longer climbs to the summit of Mount Spokane are available for this hike. We chose the Bald Knob picnic area for its scenic beauty and the fact that the primitive campground there is one of the best deals in Washington and an excellent base camp for exploring all of the trails in Mount Spokane State Park.

Begin by crossing Summit Road to the west and following Trail 130 as it traverses forest and open hillside below the road. Bear grass glows in the shaded forest; monkeyflower and shooting star wink in the sunshine as the trail crosses a spring seep. Look west for views of

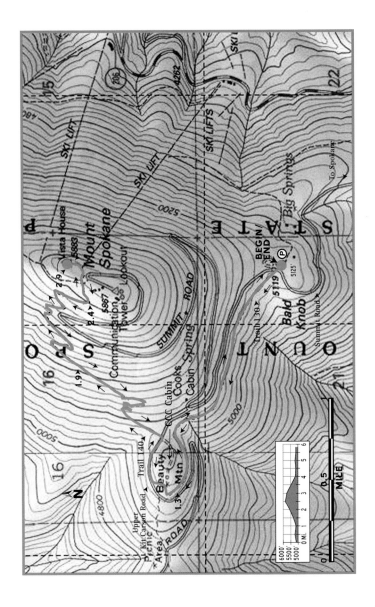

the Spokane Valley, which on some days is filled with low clouds, making it seem like you're looking down upon a field of blooming cotton.

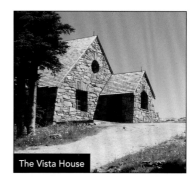
The Vista House

At **1.3** miles, you'll climb past a Civilian Conservation Corps cabin built in 1934 and reconstructed in 1998. It's a nice stop, especially in winter, where members of the Winter Knights Snowmobile Club maintain a stove and firewood supply. Next, walk west to Upper Mount Kit Carson Loop Road and turn right, hiking a few hundred yards on the road to Trail 140 on the left. You'll begin a 600-vertical-foot climb here, where the forest is young and silver snags from an old wildfire stand like exclamation points.

At **1.9** miles, the trail leaves the old burn and enters a fragrant fir forest that provides welcome shade on hot days. After a long climbing traverse, begin a series of seven switchbacks that climb around Summit Road on your right. Look to the left at **2.4** miles to a massive rock garden that probably furnished some building material for the Vista House, 0.5 mile and three switchbacks above. You'll emerge from the woods onto the paved Summit Road. To the right is a World War I memorial and viewpoint; to the left, Vista House.

PERMITS/CONTACT
Discover Pass required/Mount Spokane State Park,
(509) 238-4258, www.parks.wa.gov

MAPS
USGS Mt. Spokane; excellent PDF trail map from Friends of Mount
Spokane State Park, www.mountspokane.org

TRAIL NOTES
Leashed dogs OK; bikes and equestrians welcome

The view from the summit of Mount Spokane includes Spirit Lake in Idaho

The two-story structure is a masterpiece of stone and timberwork, where on summer weekends and holidays, hikers and motorists can get a snack or simply enjoy the 360-degree view that includes at least nine different lake basins. The most prominent is Spirit Lake, with its two islands, directly east of the mountain. In 2016, Eagle Scout Ashton Finnoe added new steel stairs to make the second-story fire lookout accessible to the public for the first time in decades.

Vista House is also the site where, on New Year's Eve in 1957, two skiers who should have known better—I'm not naming names— side-stepped up the mountain to spend the night. They made first tracks the next morning in fresh powder. Follow your own tracks back to the trailhead when you've seen everything there is to see.

Going Farther

For a longer hike and climb of about 1,300 vertical feet, begin at the big parking area east of the intersection of Mount Spokane Park Drive and Summit Road. Follow Trails 131 and 130 past the Bald Knob picnic area and campground for a round-trip hike of about 8 miles. For even longer treks to the summit, consult Mount Spokane State Park maps and information. ■

34. Quartz Mountain Lookout

RATING	DISTANCE	HIKING TIME
★ ★ ★ ★ ☆	4.8 miles round-trip	3 hours

ELEVATION GAIN	HIGH POINT	DIFFICULTY
840 feet	5,160 feet	◆ ◆ ◆ ◇ ◇

BEST MONTHS
Jan Feb Mar Apr May **Jun Jul Aug Sep Oct** Nov Dec

The Hike

Walk along wide cross-country ski and mountain bike trails through subalpine forest to a fire lookout, which is available for rent during the summer.

Getting There

Drive east on Interstate 90 to exit 287 and turn left onto Argonne Road. Follow Argonne, which joins Bruce Road, for about 8.5 miles to a round-about at Mount Spokane Park Drive (State Route 206). Follow Mount Spokane Park Drive for about 13 miles to Mount Spokane State Park. The park is open from 6:30 a.m. to dusk. Drive 3 miles to a large parking area on the right at the Summit Road intersection and turn right into the parking area. Follow the road at the east end of the parking area to a junction and keep right, driving uphill to a second lot at the Selkirk Lodge (closed in summer), 4,640 feet above sea level. Restrooms are available.

PERMITS/CONTACT
Discover Pass required/Mount Spokane State Park,
(509) 238-4258, www.parks.wa.gov

MAPS
USGS Mt. Spokane; excellent PDF trail map from Friends of Mount
Spokane State Park, www.mountspokane.org

TRAIL NOTES
Leashed dogs OK; bikes and equestrians welcome

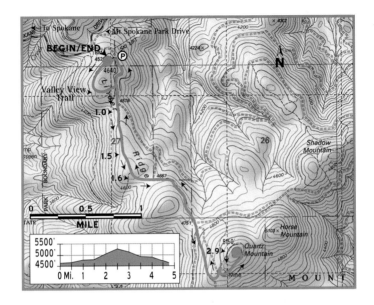

The Trail

Linder Ridge is riddled with bike and cross-country ski trails, which is a good thing because no matter how many cars are parked at the trailhead, you may not see anyone on the trail you choose. And your initial choices of trails are many because they basically all lead to the same place.

There's a big trail map at the trailhead, where you can ponder your route before starting out. All trails lead to a wide, grassy meadow at Junction 1, **0.5** mile from the trailhead if you take the Valley View Trail. From Junction 1, we chose Alpine Trail 210, which climbs into the forest before dropping back to a second meadow at Junction 2, **1.0** mile from Selkirk Lodge. Other trail options from the first junction include Blue Jay and Sam's Swoop.

At Junction 2, find Lodgepole Trail 220 and follow it to the left to Junction 3, which is about **1.5** miles from the trailhead. Look uphill to the right to see the Nova Hut, a nice warming shelter in winter or

The view from Quartz Mountain Lookout

during summer thunderstorms. Follow Lodgepole to the right, passing an old lookout trail before reaching a junction with Trail 20 at **1.6** miles, which leads to the left uphill to the Quartz Mountain Lookout.

Follow Trail 20 as it climbs in forest to a wide meadow and site of an old mine with expansive views to the south of the Spokane Valley and mountains beyond. The lookout, which was relocated from

Mount Spokane, is directly above you to the north. The trail circles Quartz Mountain and climbs steeply to the northeast before reaching the summit.

The lookout is extremely popular with renters in the summer, but if it isn't occupied or the occupants invite you, climb the steps to the catwalk and enjoy the view. To the north is Mount Spokane; to the east and south, the Spokane Valley, Mica Peak, and the basins holding Twin, Hauser, and Newman Lakes. Return the way you came, or explore other trails leading back to the trailhead.

Going Farther

The easiest way to get a longer hike is to begin from the Bald Knob campground, located 1 mile up Summit Road from the trailhead. It's an excellent and affordable base camp for exploring all the delightful trails around Mount Spokane State Park. Follow Trails 130, 132, and 131 back downhill to the Selkirk Lodge trailhead for a round-trip hike to the lookout of 6.8 miles. ■

DISTANT HIKES

35. Pend Oreille County Park

RATING	DISTANCE	HIKING TIME
★★☆☆☆	**4.1 miles round-trip**	**2.5 hours**

ELEVATION GAIN	HIGH POINT	DIFFICULTY
720 feet	**2,760 feet**	◆◆◇◇◇

BEST MONTHS
Jan Feb Mar Apr **May Jun Jul Aug Sep** Oct Nov Dec

The Hike

Here's a pleasant, shady walk through forests both old and new, featuring peekaboo views of the green valleys below.

Getting There

Drive east on Interstate 90 to exit 281 for Division Street and go north on Division, crossing the Spokane River. Follow Division as it becomes one-way north on Ruby Street before rejoining Division, designated US Routes 2 and 395. Continue downhill to the Y intersection and keep to the right on US Route 2. Drive about 26 miles to Pend Oreille County Park north of Eloika Lake and turn left to the park entrance and trailhead. The road to campgrounds in the park may be gated—the park is open from Memorial Day weekend through Labor Day weekend. Park in the lot off the highway, where you'll find a restroom and the trailhead, 2,280 feet above sea level.

PERMITS/CONTACT
None required/Pend Oreille County Department of Community Development, (509) 447-4821, www.pendoreilleco.org

MAPS
USGS Elk; downloadable county map

TRAIL NOTES
Leashed dogs OK; bikes and equestrians welcome

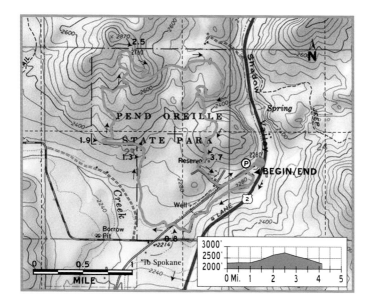

The Trail

Blame those crazy French-Canadian voyageurs for the name of the county and park, Pend Oreille, and for the pronunciation, which is absolutely nothing like "Pend Or Ellee." Say "Pondoray," instead. *Pend d'oreilles* is French for "hangs from ears," which describes the shell earrings worn by members of the Kalispel Tribe.

The trail, named Orion's Path, begins on the south side of the road in thick trees near the entrance to the park. As you probably know, Orion is the name of a Greek hunter who became a constellation, but I am quite certain he never used this trail. I'd also guess you know that one of the brightest stars in the Orion constellation is Betelgeuse, which the movie *Beetlejuice* was named for and whose producer was a poor speller. Feel free to check my research on this.

Orion's Path meanders in thick pines and fir along a hillside above the highway and below the park entrance road. After **0.8** mile, the trail turns west and joins the old road. Turn left and walk about 100 feet

Hiking a Pend Oreille County Park trail

on the road to the trail on the right. The broad pathway enters woods and a brushy understory of ocean spray. In another 0.1 mile, take the single-track trail to the left and begin climbing into older forest, **1.3** miles from the trailhead. Noise from US Route 2 below begins to diminish as you round a ridge to the west side at **1.9** miles.

The route now climbs more steeply to the north, first following the crest of a ridge, then turning into a broad gully to the west. At **2.5** miles, you'll reach a rocky viewpoint and the highest point on the trail. From here, you'll begin to drop steeply down to the east, passing several numbered trail junctions along the way. Keep right until Junction 6, turn left, and then turn right at Junction 5, which is **3.7** miles from the trailhead.

Stay left at Junction 4 and drop into a cedar grove above the campground to the campground road, turn left, and follow it to the entrance road. Take a left on the entrance road to return to the trailhead. ■

36. Bead Lake

RATING	DISTANCE	HIKING TIME
★★★★☆	10.2 miles round-trip	5 hours

ELEVATION GAIN	HIGH POINT	DIFFICULTY
1,925 feet	3,160 feet	◆◆◆◇◇

BEST MONTHS
Jan Feb Mar Apr **May Jun Jul Aug Sep** Oct Nov Dec

The Hike

Take this wonderful lakeshore trek nearly any time of year, but enjoy it most in summer, when you can take a dip in its clean, cold water and see the surrounding mountains at their emerald best.

Getting There

Drive east on Interstate 90 to exit 281 for Division Street and go north on Division, crossing the Spokane River. Follow Division as it becomes one-way north on Ruby Street before rejoining Division, designated US Routes 2 and 395. Continue downhill to the Y intersection and keep to the right on US Route 2.

Drive about 48 miles to Newport and follow US Route 2 through town to the bridge across the Pend Oreille River. Cross the bridge and take the first left onto LeClerc Road. Follow LeClerc for 2.7 miles to Bead Lake Road and turn right. Drive 6.1 miles to Bead Lake Ridge Road (Forest Road 3215) and turn right up a steep hill. Follow Bead Lake Ridge Road for 0.5 mile to a parking area on the right and the trailhead at 3,040 feet. There are no fees to park here.

An alternate trailhead and restroom are located below at the boat launch, where a fee is charged during spring and summer.

The Trail

An interesting phenomenon occurs as you drive north and east from Spokane: it begins to look more and more like the wet western side of the state. In fact, Bead Lake gets about 8 more inches of rain than Spokane's 17 inches, which can be summed up in one word: glug.

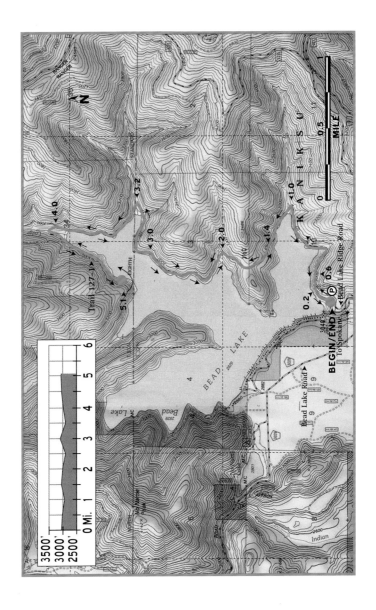

PERMITS/CONTACT
None required/Colville National Forest, Newport Ranger District,
(509) 447-7300, www.fs.usda.gov/colville

MAPS
USGS Bead Lake; National Forest map

TRAIL NOTES
Leashed dogs OK; bikes and equestrians welcome

It seemed, when B. B. Hardbody and I took this hike in July 2016, that most of the 2 feet of rain that falls every year at Bead Lake sloshed from the sky that very day.

At the trailhead, B. B. stepped out of the car into a big mud puddle I cleverly arranged to place under her door. This set the tone for the rest of the hike, which began by crossing Bead Lake Ridge Road and switching back down to a double-track road, Trail 127, at **0.2** mile that leads into the forest and back to the boat launch and restrooms. B. B. attempted to get even for the puddle trap by snapping wet cedar bows at me. (Note: After nearly four decades of hiking on the soggy side of Washington, I have learned to always let your partner walk ahead of you on rainy days so they can shake most of the rain off the leaves and branches as they pass. As with driving, don't follow too closely.)

Continuing on, turn right on Trail 127, which thins to a single trail and passes above a lakeside campsite at **0.6** mile. The trail contours about 40 feet above the lake and would be easy walking except for the fact I had to avoid stepping on burbot—freshwater lingcod that live in Bead Lake—that I'm almost certain I saw swimming on the trail. At **1.0** mile, you'll pass Enchantment Camp, which on that particular day was enchantingly drowning.

At **1.4** miles, the mud way turned uphill to climb over a forested saddle above another soggy campsite on the lake below. I opened my trusty pocket umbrella to discover it covered roughly half the circumference necessary to keep my old bald head dry. At the saddle, B. B. noted it was like a miniature Continental Divide: water flowed

A rainy day along the Bead Lake trail

south on one side and north on the other. Drop down to another campsite and creek, **2.0** miles from the trailhead.

Beyond, the route climbs along a bluff above the lake with good views of what would be No Name Peak across the lake (if we could have seen across the lake). The path then descends to lake level, which on most summer days would be excellent swimming, but it was **3.0** miles from our more enticing, warm, dry car.

Just before crossing what seemed to us like a raging lahar of Mosquito Creek, **3.2** miles from the trailhead, we looked uphill to view a Really Big Pine Tree but couldn't see that far through the fog. You'll round a point at **3.4** miles and follow the shoreline to Lodge Creek Camp at **4.0** miles. Just beyond the camp is Trail 127-1; turn left and walk another 1.1 miles to where the path ends at your turn-around spot. At that point on our hike, we considered swimming back to the trailhead via the lake, which might have been drier. ■

37. Kamiak Butte

RATING	DISTANCE	HIKING TIME
★★★ ☆ ☆	3.3 miles round-trip	2 hours
ELEVATION GAIN	**HIGH POINT**	**DIFFICULTY**
740 feet	3,641 feet	♦ ♦ ♦ ◇ ◇

BEST MONTHS											
Jan	Feb	Mar	Apr	May	Jun	Jul	Aug	Sep	Oct	Nov	Dec

The Hike

The Kamiak Butte loop trail is a short but relatively steep climb through forest to a view overlooking the rolling, verdant hills of the Palouse.

Getting There

Drive west on Interstate 90 to exit 279 for US Route 195 and go south. Drive 59 miles south to Colfax and continue through town to Canyon Street (State Route 272). Turn left, follow Canyon up the hill for 5.3 miles to Clear Creek Road, and turn right. Follow Clear Creek Road for a little more than 8 miles to Fugate Road and take a hard right. Drive a half-mile to the Kamiak Butte County Park entrance and turn left, following the road uphill to the picnic area, restroom, and trailhead, 2,920 feet above sea level. The park is open from 7 a.m. to dusk from spring through fall.

PERMITS/CONTACT
None required/Whitman County Parks and Recreation, (509) 397-6238, www.whitmancounty.org

MAPS
USGS Albion; county map

TRAIL NOTES
Leashed dogs OK

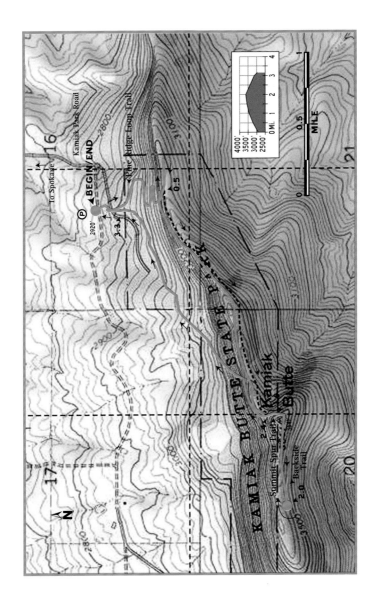

N

To Spokane

Kamiak Park Road

2800

BEGIN/END

The Ridge Loop Trail

0.5

3.3

2920'

P

2900'

0.5

KAMIAK BUTTE STATE PARK

3100'

Kamiak Butte

Summit Spur Trail

Backside Trail

2.4

2.0

3100'

2800

16

17

21

20

0Mi. 1 2 3 4

4000'
3500'
3000'
2500'

0 0.5 1

MILE

Different crops color the Palouse country below Kamiak Butte

The Trail

The path begins climbing into the forest to the south and turns left on Pine Ridge Loop Trail at a junction with your return trail. You'll be climbing about 280 feet in the span of less than a half-mile in four switchbacks to Pine Ridge, striking a trail junction at the top of the ridge **0.5** mile from the trailhead. Turn east for now, walking along the path for 0.1 mile to the park boundary to take in the broad view of the various shades of green Palouse farmland to the south.

Next, retrace your steps to the junction and stay left, climbing the sharp ridge west to Kamiak Butte. The route climbs steadily upward another 440 feet in just under a mile, reaching a junction with the Summit Spur Trail at **1.6** miles. Take the Summit Spur Trail to the left and visit the top of 3,641-foot Kamiak Butte, on private property, before dropping back to the Summit Spur Trail and turning right on the Backside Trail.

You can walk gently downhill on this trail for 0.4 mile before signs indicate you should proceed no farther on private property. Turn around and retrace your steps to the Summit Spur Trail at **2.4** miles, and turn left down through thick forest and a long, shady traverse back to the trailhead junction at **3.3** miles. ■

38. Frater Lake

RATING	DISTANCE	HIKING TIME
★★★☆☆	4.2 miles round-trip	2.5 hours
ELEVATION GAIN	**HIGH POINT**	**DIFFICULTY**
220 feet	3,433 feet	◆◆◇◇◇
BEST MONTHS		
Jan Feb Mar Apr May **Jun Jul Aug Sep** Oct Nov Dec		

The Hike

It's worth the long drive to walk the Coyote Rock Trail around Frater Lake to take in its natural beauty, fragrant forests, and wildlife-viewing opportunities.

Getting There

Drive east on Interstate 90 to exit 281 for Division Street and go north on Division, crossing the Spokane River. Follow Division as it becomes one-way north on Ruby Street before rejoining Division, designated Highways 2 and 395. Continue downhill to the Y intersection and keep to the right on US Route 2. Drive 30 miles to a junction with State Route 211 and turn left.

Follow SR 211 for 15 miles to a junction with State Route 20 at the community of Usk and turn left, passing through Cusick and driving another 28 miles to Tiger. Turn left at Tiger and continue on SR 20 for 6.4 miles to a pullout parking area and trailhead, 3,230 feet above

---

PERMITS/CONTACT
None required/Colville National Forest, Three Rivers Ranger District, (509) 684-3711, www.fs.usda.gov/colville

MAPS
USGS Alladin Mountain; National Forest map

TRAIL NOTES
Leashed dogs OK

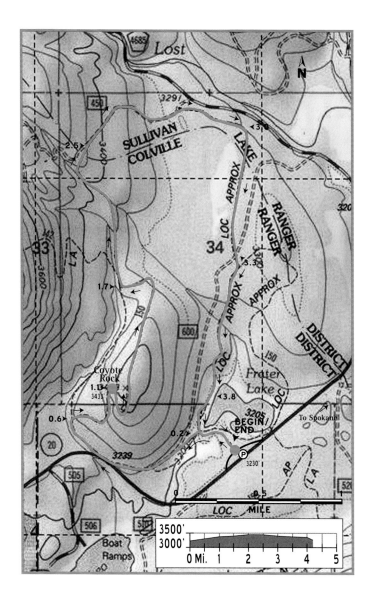

The warming hut at Frater Lake

sea level. There's a restroom and kiosk with a trail map at this designated Sno-Park area.

The Trail

This is one of the most distant hikes outlined in this guide, but if you have time for the 90-minute drive from Spokane, you shouldn't miss it. The trail is gently graded, a plus for cross-country skiers and antique outdoorsfolk like me. It meanders through a forest that is entirely different from that you'll encounter closer to the city. Tamaracks, those splendid deciduous conifers whose needles turn golden in the fall, flourish here. And you're on the edge of grizzly bear territory, where at least two wolf packs roam.

Take a look at the kiosk for information, then head toward the lake and walk along the southern shoreline to Coot Junction, which B. B. Hardbody suggested could have been named for me, "except they should add 'Old' to the name." Very funny. This section of the route is open to motorized traffic.

You'll reach the junction in **0.2** mile and turn left on a foot trail that parallels the highway on a forested hillside. At **0.6** mile, round a wide switchback and begin climbing more steeply along the hillside, passing a couple of nifty wooden barriers we imagined would be most

Frater Lake

welcome by out-of-control cross-country skiers barreling down the trail. (Note: I know something about barreling out of control on cross-country skis and am the only living person I know who once left a full body print on a chunk of avalanche debris at Mount Rainier.)

The route negotiates five switchbacks before climbing under Coyote Rock, the high point of your hike, on the left. A way trail leads to the top of the rock, polished smooth by an ancient glacier, **1.1** miles from the trailhead. The path now descends along a wide, timbered ridge to a junction with Trail 142 at **1.7** miles. Stay right and follow the path as it begins climbing again and crosses a seasonal creek that feeds Frater Lake.

You'll contour across a hillside to a wide double-track path and turn right, heading downhill **2.5** miles from the trailhead, passing several big tamaracks along the way. It was in this very forest and hike where we—being relative hiking neophytes in grizland—were certain we heard *Ursus arctos horribilis* in the woods beside the trail. We fumbled for our Counter Assault, but before we could drench the unseen monster about to eat us, a cow ambled from the understory, took one look at us, and crashed back into the woods.

Leave the double track as you approach a road paralleling Lost Creek at **3.0** miles, cross a clearing and campsite, and turn right at a trail fork, **3.3** miles from the trailhead. A diamond trail marker signifies the route at the southwest corner of a clearing leading to Scudder Junction. Head right here to a beautiful warming hut dedicated to Colville National Forest worker Guy McKee. The hut overlooks a picnic area and Frater Lake at **3.8** miles. From here, keep right around the lake to (Old) Coot Junction at **3.9** miles and turn left to the trailhead.

Going Farther

One of the best ways to get a longer walk is to park—or better yet, camp—at Lake Leo, a great little Colville National Forest campground that is 1.7 one-way miles by trail west of Frater Lake. To get there, continue west on SR 20 for 0.9 mile to the campground entrance on the left. ■

URBAN
COEUR D'ALENE

39. Tubbs Hill Loop

RATING	DISTANCE	HIKING TIME
★★★★☆	**2.4 miles round-trip**	**1.5 hours**

ELEVATION GAIN	HIGH POINT	DIFFICULTY
260 feet	**2,275 feet**	♦◇◇◇◇

BEST MONTHS
Jan Feb **Mar Apr May Jun Jul Aug Sep Oct** Nov Dec

The Hike

This popular walk is an easy stroll around a natural area that has given Coeur d'Alene residents and visitors a chance to get outdoors for more than five decades.

Getting There

From Interstate 90, take exit 13 for 4th Street, turn right, and keep right onto 3rd Street, which is one way south. Drive south to downtown Coeur d'Alene and turn left on Sherman Avenue. Follow Sherman east to South 11th Street and turn right. Continue on 11th to East Mountain Avenue and turn right. Drive past South 10th Place on your right to South 10th Street and hang a hard left. Turn right into the Eastside Park trailhead and parking area, 2,160 feet above sea level. You'll also find restrooms, a playground, and a Tubbs Hill trail marker.

An Idaho Citylink bus passes Eastside Park. For route maps and information, visit IdahoCitylink.com

---

PERMITS/CONTACT
None required/Coeur d'Alene Parks Department,
(208) 769-2252, www.cdaidparks.org

MAPS
USGS Coeur d'Alene; online city map

TRAIL NOTES
Leashed dogs OK

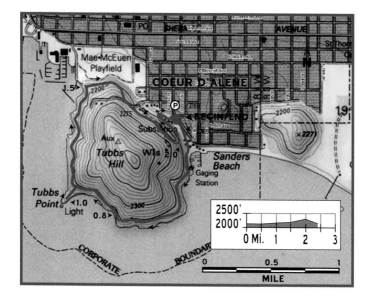

The Trail

Tubbs Hill is named for Tony A. Tubbs, who platted the west side of the hill in 1884 and was the first justice of the peace in Coeur d'Alene. The entire 120 acres of Tubbs Hill wasn't consolidated into one park until 1969, about eight years after a beer-besotted college kid—I won't say who—fell off a high rock on Tubbs Hill into the lake and nearly drowned.

The best thing about Tubbs Hill is that you can't possibly get lost. Simply keep walking along a trail around the shoreline and sooner or later you'll return to your starting point. The Eastside Park trailhead is suggested here because it isn't usually quite as crowded as Mae McEuen Playfield downtown. Begin by walking southeast along a paved walkway and climbing above the 11th Street Marina on a wide trail. You'll pass trail junctions almost every 0.2 mile, and for the longest hike, stay left on the widest main trail as you circumnavigate the hill clockwise. If you're here in the spring, the hillside is cloaked in

The Coeur d'Alene Resort is a short walk from Tubbs Hill

wildflowers and you may see that the types of blossoms change as you circle from a shady northeastern side to a sunny southwestern side.

At **0.8** mile, look uphill to an overhanging rock cave, and in another 0.2 mile, turn left for a side trip down to Corbin (Tubbs) Point, named for railroad and steamboat pioneer D. C. Corbin. Climb back to the main trail and turn right, passing a trail down to Mae McEuen Playfield and Coeur d'Alene City Hall at **1.5** miles. This is a good trail access point for guests staying at the splendid Coeur d'Alene Resort. Just beyond, climb to a crossing of Tubbs Hill Drive and continue uphill to a junction with the summit trail. Turn left on the loop trail and continue another 0.5 mile to a cutoff trail to the left, your return path to the trailhead.

Going Farther

You can combine this hike with Tubbs Hill Summit (Hike 40) for a 4.5-mile hike. Another idea: walk a half-mile northwest to Mae McEuen Playfield past the resort to the city park and return along Sherman Avenue, where nobody will complain if you stop at any of the great pubs or restaurants in order to become slightly beer-besotted yourself. ■

40. Tubbs Hill Summit

RATING	DISTANCE	HIKING TIME
★★★★	2.1 miles round-trip	1.5 hours

ELEVATION GAIN	HIGH POINT	DIFFICULTY
390 feet	2,530 feet	♦♦

BEST MONTHS
Jan Feb **Mar Apr May Jun Jul Aug Sep** Oct Nov Dec

The Hike

There's no better way to get a workout in a natural outdoor playland within the city limits of Coeur d'Alene.

Getting There

From Interstate 90, take exit 13 for 4th Street, turn right, and keep right onto 3rd Street, which is one way south. Drive south to downtown Coeur d'Alene and turn left on Sherman Avenue. Follow Sherman east to South 11th Street and turn right. Continue on 11th to East Mountain Avenue and turn right. Drive past South 10th Place on your right to South 10th Street and hang a hard left. Turn right into the Eastside Park trailhead and parking area, 2,160 feet above sea level. You'll also find restrooms, a playground, and a Tubbs Hill trail marker.

An Idaho Citylink bus passes Eastside Park. For route maps and information, visit IdahoCitylink.com.

PERMITS/CONTACT
None required/Coeur d'Alene Parks Department,
(208) 769-2252, www.cdaidparks.org

MAPS
USGS Coeur d'Alene; online city map

TRAIL NOTES
Leashed dogs OK

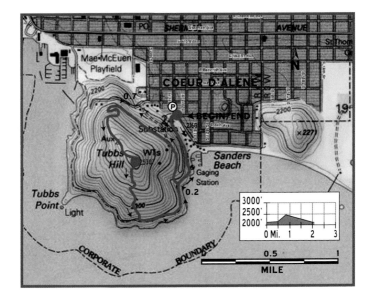

The Trail

As with the circumnavigation of Tubbs Hill Loop (Hike 39), many trails lead to the top of the hill. Some go only part of the way and disappear into a jumble of ocean spray and mean-spirited bushes with thorns, as your correspondent discovered. I sincerely hope you do not make the same mistake and that the directions here will keep you on a better path.

Begin by walking southeast along a paved path and climbing above the 11th Street Marina to the wide Tubbs Hill Loop trail at **0.2** mile; turn right, hiking in forest north above the parking area for 0.5 mile. This section is shaded, and if you're hiking in the spring, you'll likely spot trillium and glacier lilies along the way. The glacier lilies were a surprise to me; I'm accustomed to seeing them at much higher elevations. At **0.5** mile, find a trail leading steeply uphill to the left and begin some serious climbing on the Tubbs Hill Summit Trail.

A Coeur d'Alene tour boat passes under Tubbs Hill

Switchback a couple of times on the main trail, which follows the rounded ridge crest through timber to the broad, rock-strewn summit at **1.1** miles, where you'll get tree-ka-boo views of the lake and city below. When you're ready to return, walk south to find a wide trail that drops steeply to the south, crosses a fire road in 0.2 mile, and continues to plummet another 0.2 mile to the main trail around Tubbs Hill. Turn left here, following it 0.4 mile back to the junction with the trailhead path, and then turn right.

Going Farther

You can combine this hike with the Tubbs Hill Loop (Hike 39) for a 4.5-mile hike. Another idea: walk a half-mile northwest to Mae McEuen Playfield past the resort to the city park and return along Sherman Avenue, where you'll find a number of great pubs, restaurants, and shops. ■

COEUR D'ALENE SOUTHEAST

41. Mineral Ridge

RATING	DISTANCE	HIKING TIME
★★★☆☆	4.4 miles round-trip	2.5 hours

ELEVATION GAIN	HIGH POINT	DIFFICULTY
1,030 feet	3,154 feet	♦♦♦♢♢

BEST MONTHS											
Jan	Feb	Mar	Apr	**May**	**Jun**	**Jul**	**Aug**	**Sep**	Oct	Nov	**Dec**

The Hike

The climb up to Mineral Ridge is a great way to get away from the city without really driving that far and a good destination for eagle watching.

Getting There

Drive east on Interstate 90 in Coeur d'Alene to exit 22 for US Route 97 and drive 2.2 miles southwest on US 97 to the Mineral Ridge Trailhead on the left, 2,160 feet above sea level, where restrooms are available.

The Trail

This popular path is a long climb in a short distance, but well shaded for cooler hiking even on a hot summer day. On years of low snow depths, or if you're comfortable traveling on steep, snowy hillsides, this makes a good walk in December to watch the eagles that congregate below to feast on spawning kokanee in Wolf Lodge Bay. Carry traction cleats in the winter.

PERMITS/CONTACT
None required/Bureau of Land Management,
(208) 769-5000, www.blm.gov/contact/idaho

MAPS
USGS Mount Coeur d'Alene; BLM handout at trailhead kiosk

TRAIL NOTES
Leashed dogs OK

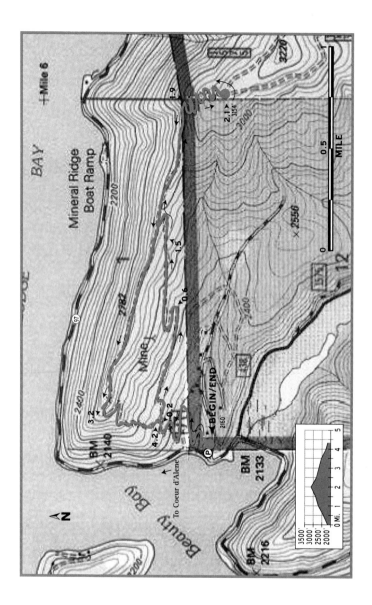

The view from the Mineral Ridge Trail

Start by climbing the steps and following the wide trail for **0.2** mile to a junction with your return trail and turn right. Switchback a couple of times and begin a long, climbing traverse in deep forest for 0.4 mile to a second set of switchbacks. Climb these to find a side trail leading to an abandoned mine in 0.1 mile. Return to the main route and make another climbing traverse to a final switchback to gain Mineral Ridge, **1.5** miles from the trailhead. We were pleasantly surprised to find a water fountain here.

The trail forks, and families with young children or those wishing to take a shorter hike can turn left and return via the Mineral Ridge Trail for a 2.7-mile loop. Caribou Cabin, a nice picnic shelter with a terrific view of Lake Coeur d'Alene, is located on the ridge crest.

For the longer hike, turn right and follow the crest of the ridge above Wolf Lodge Bay as it continues to climb for a little less than a half-mile to the Bluebird viewpoint at **1.9** miles. Another viewpoint, Silver Wave, is another 0.2 mile beyond. This is your turnaround, **2.1** miles from the trailhead.

Follow the trail back to Caribou Cabin and keep right, following the Mineral Ridge Trail past the Gray Wolf viewpoint to the Silver

Tip viewpoint overlooking Beauty Bay, **3.2** miles from the trailhead. Begin a series of steep switchbacks down to join your path up at **4.2** miles and continue down to the parking area. The lower part of this trail is trashed by switchback-cutting slobs.

Going Farther

You can hike beyond the Silver Wave viewpoint for more than 3 miles round-trip by climbing in two switchbacks to the Elk Mountain trailhead and following logging roads along the crest of Mineral Ridge. ■

42. Mount Coeur d'Alene

RATING	DISTANCE	HIKING TIME
★★★☆☆	**10.4 miles round-trip**	**6 hours**

ELEVATION GAIN	HIGH POINT	DIFFICULTY
2,300 feet	**4,439 feet**	♦♦♦♦◇

BEST MONTHS
Jan Feb Mar Apr **May Jun Jul Aug Sep Oct** Nov Dec

The Hike

The climb to Mount Coeur d'Alene along Caribou Ridge National Recreation Trail No. 79 is an exhilarating workout, with thrills and views at the start instead of at the summit.

Getting There

Drive east on Interstate 90 in Coeur d'Alene to exit 22 for US Route 97. Follow US 97 southwest for 2.5 miles to Forest Road 438 and turn left. Drive 0.7 mile to the entrance to Beauty Creek Campground, turn right, and stop at the first parking area on the right and the trailhead, 2,160 feet above sea level. A restroom is available at the campground, which makes a good base camp for hiking here and at Mineral Ridge (Hike 41).

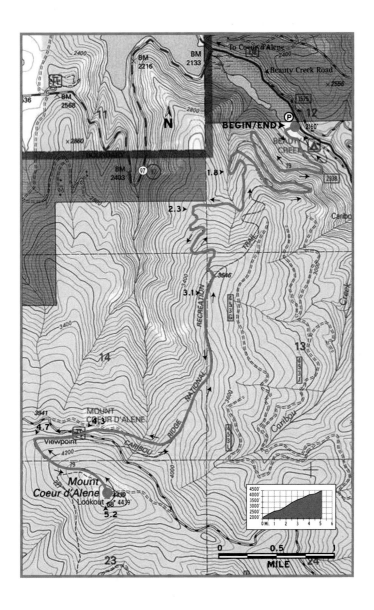

To Coeur d'Alene

Beauty Creek Road

×2558

BEGIN/END ▶

BEAUTY CREEK

1.8 ▶

2.3 ▶

Caribou

3.1 ▶ ×3646

RECREATION

14

13

MOUNT
COEUR D'ALENE
4.3 ▶
4.7 ◀

Viewpoint

CARIBOU

RIDGE

Caribou Creek

79

Mount
Coeur d'Alene
Lookout 68° 4439'
5.2

23

24

4500'
4000'
3500'
3000'
2500'
2000'

0 Mi. 1 2 3 4 5 6

0   0.5   1
MILE

The Trail

If you are the sort of person who resents putting sweat equity into a trek only to find you could have motored merrily to the same location, you might not want to make this strenuous climb. On the other hand, if you are happy to see a place in the wildland that can be accessed by those who can't get there on foot, you should enjoy this walk.

We would have enjoyed it immensely, if only your acrophobic correspondent could have refrained from whining and whimpering along the fairly steep and exposed lower trail. I am surprised B. B. Hardbody didn't bump me off a cliff. We call that a "Montana divorce," after the 2014 case in Glacier National Park where a newlywed bride bodychecked her husband to his death.

Begin by walking south on the grassy Beauty Creek floodplain and crossing the creek bed before entering the sparse forest on the opposite bank. The trail begins to climb immediately on a moderate grade, switching back five times and gaining almost 800 feet in the first mile. The path crosses open cliff bands with views of the campground below and Beauty Bay to the northwest. The first vista is **0.5** mile from the trailhead.

At **1.8** miles, the path was eroded at the fourth switchback and we found the roots of a tree made for good foot- and handholds. Climb another 0.1 mile to the final turn, where the trail enters a thicker forest and cooling shade.

Beauty Bay from the Mount Coeur d'Alene trail

You'll climb directly up a ridge before crossing a gully and climbing to a junction with a gated four-wheel-drive path on the right, **2.3** miles from the trailhead. Now the trail turns uphill again in forest, switching back six times to gain more than 500 feet in the next half-mile. At **3.1** miles, find a junction with Trail No. 258 and bear right. From here, the path climbs up a ridge crest in a thinning forest now decorated with bear grass.

At **4.3** miles, climb to FR 439 and cross it to the west to the Mount Coeur d'Alene picnic area, where you'll find a restroom and water from a spring. The trail to the summit begins at the picnic area on a climbing traverse to the west and arrives at a junction with Trail No. 227, **4.7** miles from the trailhead. Keep left and continue climbing to the broad summit of Mount Coeur d'Alene, your turnaround spot at **5.2** miles. A lookout tower was once located here but today you'll find a metal shack used mainly for target practice by jerks. ∎

43. Lakeshore Loop, Heyburn State Park

RATING	DISTANCE	HIKING TIME
★★★ ☆☆	**4.2 miles round-trip**	**2.5 hours**

ELEVATION GAIN	HIGH POINT	DIFFICULTY
320 feet	**2,260 feet**	◆ ◇ ◇ ◇ ◇

BEST MONTHS
Jan Feb Mar **Apr May Jun Jul Aug Sep** Oct Nov Dec

The Hike

This quiet nature trail along the shore of Chatcolet Lake shows off everything from aquatic birds to moose, wildflowers in season, and a beautiful mature cedar forest.

Getting There

Take exit 12 from Interstate 90 in Coeur d'Alene and turn right on US Route 95 (Lincoln Way). Follow US 95 south for 31 miles to Plummer, Idaho, and turn left on State Route 5. Follow SR 5 for 6.4 miles to Heyburn State Park Visitor Center and Hawleys Landing Campground and turn left. If you don't have one, you can purchase a required motor vehicle entry fee ($5 per day in 2017) at the visitor center. Turn left at the visitor center on Chatcolet Road and drive 1.1 miles to the Indian Cliffs parking area and trailhead on the left, just across the Trail of the Coeur d'Alenes, 2,180 feet above sea level.

PERMITS/CONTACT
Vehicle fee required/Heyburn State Park, (208) 686-1308,
www.parksandrecreation.idaho.gov/parks/heyburn

MAPS
USGS Chatcolet; Heyburn State Park map

TRAIL NOTES
Leashed dogs OK

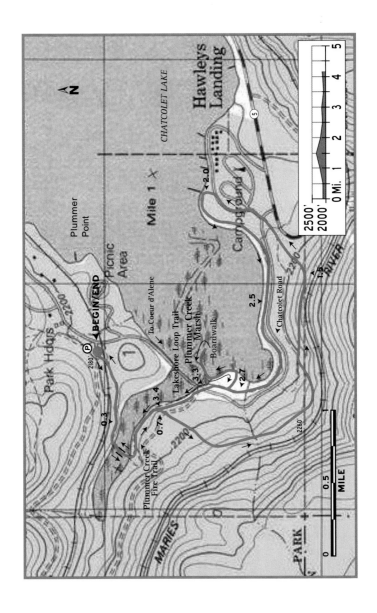

N

CHATCOLET LAKE

Hawley's
Landing

Plummer
Point

Mile 1

Picnic
Area

Park Hdqts

BEGIN/END

2100'

To Coeur d'Alene

Lakeshore Loop Trail

Plummer Creek
Marsh

Boardwalk

Campground

Chatcolet Road

2200'

2200'

RIVER

2180'

0.3

0.7

3.4

3.3

2.7

2.5

2.0

1.5

5

Plummer Creek
Fire Trail

2260'

MARIES

PARK

0   0.5   MILE

2500'
2000'

0 Mi.   1   2   3   4   5

Plummer Creek flows toward Chatcolet Lake

Restrooms are located about a quarter-mile northeast on the Trail of the Coeur d'Alenes at Plummer Point.

Hikers coming from Spokane who wish to avoid the Coeur d'Alene urban area can follow I-90 east to exit 289 for Pines Road, and follow Pines south on SR 27 for about 17 miles to Rockford. Turn left and follow SR 278 through Rockford to a junction with US 95 in Idaho; go south on US 95 and follow the directions on page 157.

The Trail

This gentle trail is a good hike in late spring, after the lowland portions along the lake have dried out a bit and trillium and skunk cabbage color the cedar-forest understory. It's a popular path for hikers and bikers making a base camp at Hawleys Landing Campground, with its easy paved road or trail access to the Trail of the Coeur d'Alenes.

Begin by crossing the Trail of the Coeur d'Alenes and finding the trail heading west into the pine forest and a junction with the Appaloosa Trail at **0.3** mile. Turn left and cross a bridge over Plummer

Creek, where you might see anything from beaver or muskrat to a moose splashing around in the creek. Just across the bridge, climb to the Plummer Creek Fire Trail and stay left on the Plummer Creek Trail.

At **0.7** mile, find a junction with the Lakeshore Loop Trail, your return route. Turn right and climb a steep road that passes a holding pond, and stay left at the next junction, contouring above the Chatcolet Road for a half-mile. The trail turns left at **1.5** miles and drops to the Heyburn Visitor Center. Cross Hawleys Landing Campground Road and follow the signs to the tent-camping area, one of the nicest tenting areas to be found around this neck of the woods.

Follow the road down to a dock and the shoreline of Chatcolet Lake, **2.0** miles from the trailhead, and turn left along the shoreline trail. You'll pass below the visitor center and enter a beautiful cedar forest at **2.5** miles. Next, walk another 0.2 mile to the Plummer Creek Marsh and boardwalk, which takes you into a water lily garden on the lake where red-winged blackbirds rule the roost.

After cruising the boardwalk, head back to the trail and turn right, crossing the Chatcolet Road at **3.3** miles and taking the Plummer Creek Trail on the right. Walk another 0.1 mile to a junction and your return route to the right.

Going Farther

This hike can be combined with any of the other trails that begin at the Indian Cliffs Trailhead for routes totaling up to 10 miles. Another option is to walk a section of the Trail of the Coeur d'Alenes, 5 miles one-way uphill to the Plummer Trailhead, or 3.5 miles one-way to the Chatcolet Bridge. ■

44. Indian Cliffs and CCC Loops

RATING	DISTANCE	HIKING TIME
★★★★☆	3.5 miles round-trip	2 hours

ELEVATION GAIN	HIGH POINT	DIFFICULTY
680 feet	2,680 feet	◆◆◆◇◇

BEST MONTHS
Jan Feb Mar **Apr May Jun Jul Aug Sep Oct** Nov Dec

The Hike
Climb to a great view of Chatcolet Lake and the Plummer Creek slough in one of the oldest state parks in the Inland Northwest.

Getting There
Take exit 12 from Interstate 90 in Coeur d'Alene and turn right on US Route 95 (Lincoln Way). Follow US 95 south for 31 miles to Plummer, Idaho, and turn left on State Route 5. Follow SR 5 for 6.4 miles to Heyburn State Park Visitor Center and Hawleys Landing Campground and turn left. If you don't have one, you can purchase a required motor vehicle entry fee ($5 per day in 2017) at the visitor center. Turn left at the visitor center on Chatcolet Road and drive 1.1 miles to the Indian Cliffs parking area and trailhead on the left, just across the Trail of the Coeur d'Alenes, 2,180 feet above sea level. Restrooms are located about a quarter-mile northeast on the Trail of the Coeur d'Alenes at Plummer Point.

PERMITS/CONTACT
Vehicle fee required/Heyburn State Park, (208) 686-1308,
www.parksandrecreation.idaho.gov/parks/heyburn

MAPS
USGS Chatcolet; Heyburn State Park map

TRAIL NOTES
Leashed dogs OK

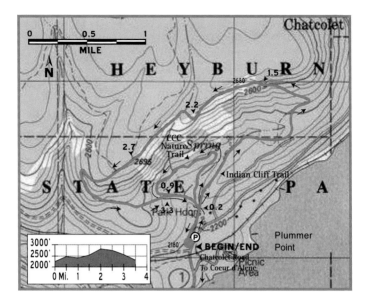

Hikers coming from Spokane who wish to avoid the Coeur d'Alene urban area can follow I-90 east to exit 289 for Pines Road, and follow Pines south on SR 27 for about 17 miles to Rockford. Turn left and follow SR 278 through Rockford to a junction with US 95 in Idaho; go south on US 95 and follow the directions on the previous page.

The Trail

Combine two loop trails into one hike for a longer stroll that gives different perspectives from the same forested hill. The first, shorter loop is named for the Civilian Conservation Corps, which established a camp at Heyburn State Park. From 1934 to 1938, CCC workers built roads in the park and laid a pipeline across Chatcolet Lake to Rocky Point, and they built both the trails you're walking today.

Begin by finding the trail at the northeast end of the parking area and climbing into the forest. At **0.2** mile, you'll strike a junction with the Indian Cliffs Trail and keep to the left on the CCC Trail. This path circles through a lowland forest where different trees compete for sun and water, yielding welcome shade on hot summer days. Critters chewed holes in the brochure we found at the trailhead, but we can tell you from the remnants we were able to identify trees such as the wes(hole)n larch, gra(tiny hole) fir, and p(big hole)osa pine.

The view from Indian Cliffs

At **0.9** mile, reach a junction with the Indian Cliffs Trail and turn left to close the loop. Next, turn left on the Indian Cliffs Trail and begin a longer climb to the flat bench above the cliffs. The route grows increasingly steeper, eventually climbing 360 vertical feet in less than a mile and switching back once. Once on the bench, the view opens up, and you can look across to Hawleys Landing Campground and down to the mouth of Plummer Creek.

You'll pass a trail leading to a viewpoint at **1.5** miles and stay right for another 0.7 mile to a point where the trail turns left toward Indian Cliffs. At **2.7** miles, arrive at a junction with a shortcut leading to the Whitetail Loop Trail, and find a sign and picnic table at the Indian Cliffs viewpoint. Stay left and begin a descent through open forest, switching back once and dropping to a junction with the CCC Trail at **3.3** miles. Stay right and arrive at the trailhead in another 0.2 mile.

Going Farther

Perhaps the best option for extending this walk is to hike a portion of the Trail of the Coeur d'Alenes, just below the parking area. This paved path curves northeast for about 3.5 miles one-way to a bridge crossing at Chatcolet, or 5.5 miles one-way uphill to the Plummer Trailhead. Plummer Point, where you'll find a picnic area, restrooms, and a swimming beach, is less than 1 mile northeast on the trail. ∎

45. Whitetail Loop

RATING	DISTANCE	HIKING TIME
★★☆☆☆	8.0 miles round-trip	4.5 hours
ELEVATION GAIN	**HIGH POINT**	**DIFFICULTY**
780 feet	2,920 feet	◆◆◆◇
BEST MONTHS		
Jan Feb Mar **Apr May Jun Jul Aug Sep** Oct Nov Dec		

The Hike

Climb through open forest and an old burn along overgrown fire roads where visibility makes spotting distant deer and other wild critters easier.

Getting There

Take exit 12 from Interstate 90 in Coeur d'Alene and turn right on US Route 95 (Lincoln Way). Follow US 95 south for 31 miles to Plummer, Idaho, and turn left on State Route 5. Follow SR 5 for 6.4 miles to Heyburn State Park Visitor Center and Hawleys Landing Campground and turn left. If you don't have one, you can purchase a required motor vehicle entry fee ($5 per day in 2017) at the visitor center. Turn left at the visitor center on Chatcolet Road and drive 1.1 miles to the Indian Cliffs parking area and trailhead on the left, just across the Trail of the Coeur d'Alenes, 2,180 feet above sea level. Restrooms are located about a quarter-mile northeast on the Trail of the Coeur d'Alenes at Plummer Point.

PERMITS/CONTACT
Vehicle fee required/Heyburn State Park, (208) 686-1308,
www.parksandrecreation.idaho.gov/parks/heyburn

MAPS
USGS Chatcolet; Heyburn State Park map

TRAIL NOTES
Leashed dogs OK; bikes and equestrians welcome

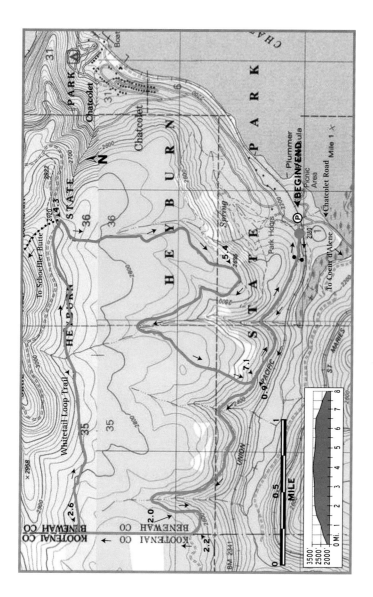

Hikers coming from Spokane who wish to avoid the Coeur d'Alene urban area can follow I-90 east to exit 289 for Pines Road, and follow Pines south on SR 27 for about 17 miles to Rockford. Turn left and follow SR 278 through Rockford to a junction with US 95 in Idaho; go south on US 95 and follow the directions on page 164.

The Trail

This wide path, an old fire road, begins at the west end of the parking area and passes a gate before climbing into open forest above

Whitetail Loop Trail

the paved Trail of the Coeur d'Alenes. It parallels the trail, climbing higher above it at every bend, for 0.9 mile, where you'll find a junction with your return route. Stay left and continue a steady climb along a south-facing hillside, rounding a couple of wide gullies with seasonal streams.

At the west side of the second gully, find a junction with the Whitetail horse trail at **2.0** miles, and turn right up a steeper section of the path to a fire road and fence line at **2.2** miles. Turn right on the fence line, which is the boundary between Benewah and Kootenai Counties, and follow the fire road past a sign that indicated a trail we couldn't find in the overgrown brush, **2.6** miles from the trailhead. Continue on the obvious fire road for another 0.2 mile to a junction with the Whitetail Loop and Schoeffler Butte Trails and turn right.

The route now traverses open forest where you can look down a brushy, gentle slope that makes wildlife watching easier. It climbs at a gentle pace for more than a mile to a second trail leading uphill to Schoeffler Butte, **4.3** miles from the trailhead. Turn right here and follow a single track downhill along a gully and descend to a junction with the short trail leading to the Indian Cliffs viewpoint at **5.4** miles.

If you've stopped at Indian Cliffs for the view—the best on this hike—return to the Whitetail Loop Trail and turn left. The path drops into a wide draw and rounds the headwaters of a seasonal creek before dropping and switching back to join your return route at **7.1** miles. Turn left and walk 0.9 mile to the parking area.

Going Farther

The loop trail up and over Schoeffler Butte is 3.8 miles. Turn left at the second junction with the Whitetail Loop Trail, 4.3 miles from the trailhead. Besides the extra mileage, you'll climb an additional 400 vertical feet. ■

46. Trail of the Coeur d'Alenes, Plummer Point–Hndarep

RATING ★★☆☆☆	DISTANCE 8.0 miles round-trip	HIKING TIME 4 hours
ELEVATION GAIN 80 feet	HIGH POINT 2,260 feet	DIFFICULTY ◆◆◇◇◇
BEST MONTHS Jan Feb Mar **Apr May Jun Jul Aug Sep Oct** Nov Dec		

The Hike

Families, wheelchair hikers, leashed dogs—all who use muscle power to move, in fact—will enjoy the Trail of the Coeur d'Alenes, any time of the year.

Getting There

Take exit 12 from Interstate 90 in Coeur d'Alene and turn right on US Route 95 (Lincoln Way). Follow US 95 south for 31 miles to Plummer, Idaho, and turn left on State Route 5. Follow SR 5 for 6.4 miles to

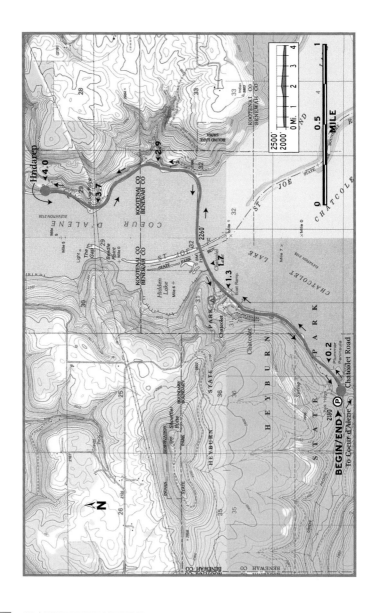

Heyburn State Park Visitor Center and Hawleys Landing Campground
and turn left. If you don't have one, you can purchase a required
motor vehicle entry fee ($5 per day in 2017) at the visitor center. Turn
left at the visitor center on Chatcolet Road and drive 1.1 miles to the
Indian Cliffs parking area and trailhead on the left, just across the
Trail of the Coeur d'Alenes, 2,180 feet above sea level. Restrooms
are located about a quarter-mile northeast on the Trail of the Coeur
d'Alenes at Plummer Point.

Hikers coming from Spokane who wish to avoid the Coeur d'Alene
urban area can follow I-90 east to exit 289 for Pines Road, and follow
Pines south on SR 27 for about 17 miles to Rockford. Turn left and
follow SR 278 through Rockford to a junction with US 95 in Idaho; go
south on US 95 and follow the directions on page 167.

The Trail

The abandoned route of the Union Pacific Railroad is today among
the very best walking, biking, inline skating, and wheelchair-accessible
pathways in America. It stretches for more than 72 miles from Plummer
to Mullan, Idaho, passing through farmland and wildland along one
of the most scenic rivers in the nation. Cross-country skiers, snowshoe
hikers, and fat-tire bicyclists leave tracks in the winter. But no matter
the season, the chance to spot wildlife is excellent and the scenery
tough to beat.

Sections of the route are managed by different agencies, and
the portion you walk today is maintained by the Coeur d'Alene

Tribe, Idaho Department of Transportation, and Idaho State Parks and Recreation. The Coeur d'Alene Tribe has named many of the rest areas and stops along the way, including Hndarep—"canoe landing"—and numerous interpretive signs along the trail provide a rich history of the first people who lived here. Begin by taking the short path down to the trail from the parking area, undoubtedly the steepest and roughest 30 feet of this hike, and turning northeast on the trail.

You'll pass Heyburn State Park rental cabins on your left and thick forest on your right before arriving at a rest stop at Plummer Point at **0.2** mile. A picnic area and swimming beach here make a good spot to cool off after a summer walk. Beyond, the route follows the shoreline of Chatcolet Lake to the community of Chatcolet, where you'll find a primitive campground and picnic area, restrooms, and a large parking area and trailhead, **1.3** miles from the trailhead.

Pass a marina and boat launch on your right and walk another 0.4 mile to the main attraction on this route: the Chatcolet railroad bridge. Originally a level span that swung open in the middle for boat traffic, the center portion—the highest point of your hike—was raised and new decking installed in steps for pedestrians and cyclists. The bridge is 3,100 feet long and divides Chatcolet Lake, on the right, from Lake Coeur d'Alene, on the left.

The route on the other side of the bridge turns north along the lakeshore and passes a marshy inlet at **2.9** miles, where great blue herons are often spotted trying to catch a frog dinner. Next, round St. Joe Point at **3.7** miles, and walk another 0.3 mile to Hndarep, your turnaround point, where you'll find picnic tables and a restroom.

Going Farther

The best way to hike farther on this section of the trail is to follow the Trail of the Coeur d'Alenes to the west, up to 5 miles one-way, to Plummer. This path is the longest climb on the entire trail and passes through beautiful old pine forest above the Plummer Creek drainage. ∎

47. Trail of the Coeur d'Alenes, Harrison–Sqwe'mu'lmkhw

RATING	DISTANCE	HIKING TIME
★★★☆☆	6.6 miles round-trip	3.5 hours

ELEVATION GAIN	HIGH POINT	DIFFICULTY
20 feet	2,170 feet	◆◇◇◇◇

BEST MONTHS
Jan Feb Mar Apr **May Jun Jul Aug Sep Oct** Nov Dec

The Hike

The walk from Harrison south along the shore of Lake Coeur d'Alene is one of the prettiest and most civilized ways to enjoy nature any time of the year.

Getting There

A number of highways lead to the trailhead in Harrison, but perhaps the easiest drive is to follow Interstate 90 east from Coeur d'Alene to exit 34 for State Route 3, then follow Highway 3 southwest for 21 miles to an intersection with State Route 97 and turn right, driving 8 miles northwest to Harrison. Turn left on West Harrison Street to find free city parking on Lake Avenue behind One Shot Charlie's, or park at the city park and campground behind the Gateway Marina, 2,170 feet above sea level. Restrooms are located on the trail and at the city campground.

PERMITS/CONTACT
None required/Coeur d'Alene Tribe Recreation Management,
(208) 686-5305

MAPS
USGS Harrison, USGS Black Lake; Trail of the Coeur d'Alenes map

TRAIL NOTES
Leashed dogs OK; bikes welcome

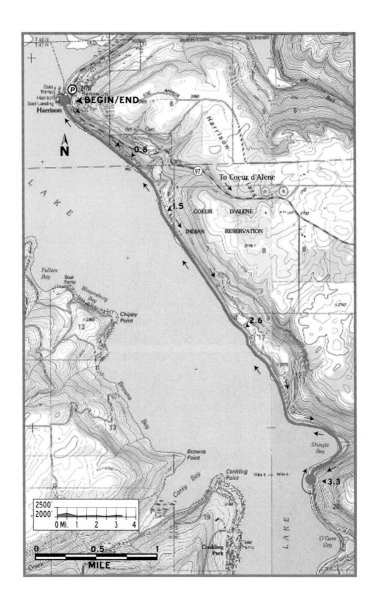

Benches offer scenic rests along the trail

The Trail

It would be difficult to find a better spot in the entire Inland Northwest to vegetate than Harrison, Idaho, on the shores of Lake Coeur d'Alene. It rocks in the summer with live music and barbecues and is a quiet, splendid retreat in the winter. One Shot Charlie's is popular with bicyclists, hikers, and motorcyclists, who mix with the boating crowd from the marina. Yet you won't find the teeming hordes of tourists you might encounter in Coeur d'Alene or Sandpoint—not that they're a bad thing (we're all tourists at one time or another).

Start by walking south along the Trail of the Coeur d'Alenes, passing the City of Harrison campground on the right, where RVs have their own lakefront sites and tent campers share a wide lawn. The hill to the east hosts houses both old and new, and rises steeply from the trail. At **0.3** mile, the paved path passes the old steamboat landing, where wild roses color the way. Here and along the entire trail, the route bisects private property; hikers are asked to respect it and stay on the path.

At **0.8** mile, one artistic resident managed to put together a praying mantis sculpture, built exclusively from what appears to be motorcycle parts, as well as an in-flight dragonfly. Past the metal bugs, traffic noise and residences on the hillside thin out, and the only noise you might hear is the lapping of waves on the shoreline.

The route is straight and level for about a mile beginning at **1.5** miles before it passes a housing development on the left, rounds a point, and then turns into Shingle Bay. Sqwe'mu'lmkhw, the rest stop that translates to "a familiar place," is in a nice shaded spot with a picnic table and restroom, **3.3** miles from the trailhead and your turnaround spot.

Going Farther

For a longer walk, you can continue for another 2.1 miles one-way to the Hndarep rest area and picnic spot, making for a round-trip hike of 10.8 miles. ■

48. Trail of the Coeur d'Alenes, Harrison–Gray's Meadow

RATING ★★★☆☆	DISTANCE 10.4 miles round-trip	HIKING TIME 5.5 hours
ELEVATION GAIN 40 feet	HIGH POINT 2,160 feet	DIFFICULTY ◆◆◆◇◇
BEST MONTHS		
Jan Feb Mar **Apr May Jun Jul Aug Sep Oct** Nov Dec		

The Hike

Tour the quiet side of the Trail of the Coeur d'Alenes, where wildlife and waterfowl are almost as common as bicycles and pedestrians.

Getting There

A number of highways lead to the trailhead in Harrison, but perhaps the easiest drive is to follow Interstate 90 east from Coeur d'Alene to exit 34 for State Route 3, then follow Highway 3 southwest for 21 miles to an intersection with State Route 97 and turn right, driving 8 miles northwest to Harrison. Turn left on West Harrison Street to find free city parking on Lake Avenue behind One Shot Charlie's, or park at the city park and campground behind the Gateway Marina, 2,170 feet above sea level. Restrooms are located on the trail and at the city campground.

The Trail

While some parts of the Trail of the Coeur d'Alenes parallel I-90 or state routes, the section from Harrison east soon leaves the highway noise behind, letting you listen to the sounds of nature as you walk between shallow lakes and along river shoreline. The pathway here is only slightly above the water table, and you'll spy numerous tracks of wild critters trailing mud across the paved route.

We'd suggest this as an evening walk, when the sun will be at your back on the way and you can watch the sunset on the return. You'll be passing through private property, so please stay on the trail.

Walk east from Harrison under a steep hillside below town for 1.3 miles to an overpass where Highway 97 turns north. From here

The Coeur d'Alene River

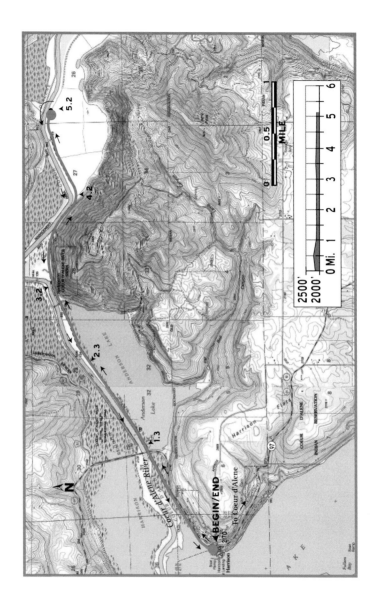

to Gray's Meadow, you'll enjoy hiking without traffic noise. It's as if some wise and benevolent agency decided to pave a hiking and biking trail in the middle of nature. In fact, they did.

You'll be walking a causeway between the main stem of the Coeur d'Alene River on the left and Anderson Lake on the right. At **3.2** miles, reach the Springston Trailhead, which is the last auto access to the trail for the next 7 miles. Picnic tables and a restroom make this a good turnaround spot for families with young children.

To continue, round a tree-shaded bluff that is part of the Coeur d'Alene River Wildlife Management Area, where you might not be surprised to see wildlife. This section of the trail is one where moose are frequently sighted. Gray's Meadow, a mile-long carpet of green, basks in sun to your right. You'll reach the wayside, with its picnic table, **5.2** miles from the trailhead.

Going Farther

Even though the round-trip hike of 10.4 miles is level as a pancake griddle, it's still a lot of miles to put on the Vibrams in a single day. Still, if you're up for a longer walk, it's 3.5 miles to the Cave Lake Wayside, making for 17.4 miles round-trip. ■

49. Trail of the Coeur d'Alenes, Medimont–Gray's Meadow

RATING	DISTANCE	HIKING TIME
★★★★☆	10.2 miles round-trip	5.5 hours

ELEVATION GAIN	HIGH POINT	DIFFICULTY
20 feet	2,140 feet	◆◆◇◇◇

BEST MONTHS
~~Jan~~ ~~Feb~~ ~~Mar~~ Apr May Jun Jul Aug Sep Oct ~~Nov~~ ~~Dec~~

The Hike

Looking to get up close and personal with a moose? This might be your best chance.

Getting There

Follow Interstate 90 east from Coeur d'Alene to exit 34 for State Route 3. Follow Highway 3 southwest for 12 miles to East Rainy Hill Road and turn right. Follow Rainy Hill for 1 mile to South Medimont Road and turn right. Drive 0.8 mile to the parking area, staying left on South Ruddy Duck Road at the Y intersection. The trailhead, 2,140 feet above sea level, has a restroom and picnic tables.

The Trail

Only pedestrians and bicyclists will be your company on this hike, unless you encounter a moose or other wildlife along the way, which

PERMITS/CONTACT
None required/Idaho Department of Parks and Recreation, (208) 682-3814, www.parksandrecreation.idaho.gov

MAPS
USGS Medimont, USGS Black Lake; Trail of the Coeur d'Alenes map

TRAIL NOTES
Leashed dogs OK; bikes welcome

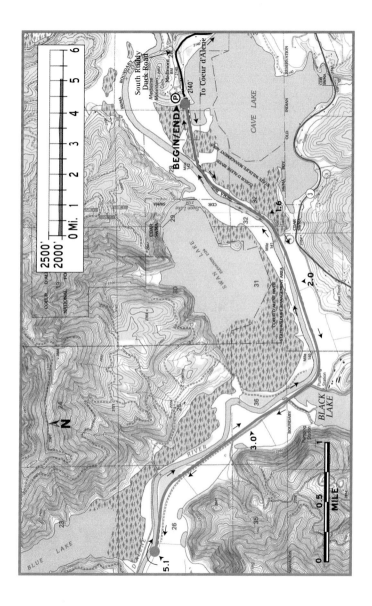

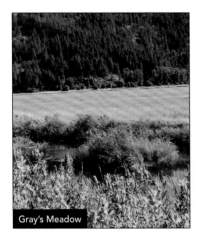
Gray's Meadow

is quite likely in this part of the Coeur d'Alene River Wildlife Management Area. Private roads parallel part of the path but see little traffic except farm vehicles. As with all the hikes along the Trail of the Coeur d'Alenes, please respect private property and stay on the trail.

We'd suggest a morning hike for this section of the trail so you'll have the sun at your back on the way out. The earlier you start, the more likely you are to spot wildlife. If you don't see a moose, you're almost certain to see its tracks. If you do see one though, give it plenty of space, especially in the spring when cows are protective and in the fall when bulls would like nothing better than to clomp all over you. You have been warned.

From Medimont, one of the old waysides of the Union Pacific Railroad, walk southwesterly along the river on your right. The route follows a causeway between the river and Cave Lake to the south. Cave Lake picnic area, **1.6** miles from the trailhead, might be the best turnaround spot for families with young hikers. Swan Lake lies to the north, which you might guess was not named for the large number of feral Pomeranians said to frequent the area. (Feel free to check my research.)

At **2.0** miles, look to the south to the white vinyl fences of beautiful Black Lake Ranch, which the Idaho Department of Fish and Game was in the process of purchasing for $2.6 million in summer of 2016. Plans for the former quarter-horse ranch call for recreational use. The trail now turns to the northwest where the river takes a bend away from the path.

The river returns to accompany the trail at **4.1** miles before the route ducks into a pine forest and enters Gray's Meadow at **5.1** miles. A picnic table, restrooms, and benches can be found here, your turnaround.

Going Farther

If you wish to hike beyond Gray's Meadow, Springston Wayside with its picnic tables, restrooms, and trailhead is another 2.4 miles one-way. That would make the round-trip from Medimont 15 miles—a long day hike, even on paved, level path. ■

50. Trail of the Coeur d'Alenes, Medimont–Lane

RATING ★★☆☆☆	DISTANCE 7.6 miles round-trip	HIKING TIME 4 hours
ELEVATION GAIN 20 feet	HIGH POINT 2,140 feet	DIFFICULTY ◆◇◇◇◇
BEST MONTHS		
Jan Feb Mar **Apr May Jun Jul Aug Sep Oct** Nov Dec		

The Hike

River and wetlands accompany you on this walk mostly lacking shade and best taken on a cloudy, cool day.

Getting There

Follow Interstate 90 east from Coeur d'Alene to exit 34 for State Route 3. Follow Highway 3 southwest for 12 miles to East Rainy Hill Road and turn right. Follow Rainy Hill for 1 mile to South Medimont Road and turn right. Drive 0.8 mile to the parking area, staying left on South Ruddy Duck Road at the Y intersection. The trailhead, 2,140 feet above sea level, has a restroom and picnic tables.

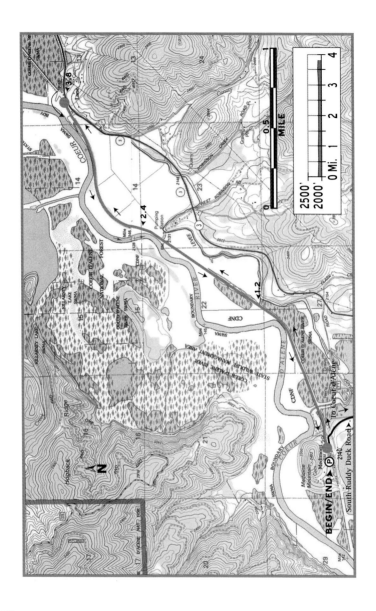

PERMITS/CONTACT
None required/Idaho Department of Parks and Recreation,
(208) 682-3814, www.parksandrecreation.idaho.gov

MAPS
USGS Medimont, USGS Lane; Trail of the Coeur d'Alenes map

TRAIL NOTES
Leashed dogs OK; bikes welcome

The Trail

The walk from Medimont to the Lane Wayside, with its restrooms and picnic tables, serves up fine opportunities for wildlife and waterfowl watching. The Coeur d'Alene River on the left and state wildlife management area wetlands on the right provide vistas almost unencumbered by trees. This has its downside on hot summer days, so we'd recommend waiting until early evening for this hike, when the sun is at your back on the way out and you can enjoy the sunset on the return. It's also one of the best times to see wildlife along the way.

Begin by walking east through a rocky cut and under the South Medimont Road bridge, which still bears dark smudges from the Union Pacific diesel and steam engines that passed this way until the 1990s. You'll cross a slow channel that drains Medicine Lake to the south between wetlands and the river, popular with anglers after panfish. At **1.2** miles, a levee along the south side of the trail keeps things a bit drier, while the river turns north away from the trail.

Beyond, the broad marsh to the north includes Killarney Lake, **2.4** miles from the trailhead. Killarney is the site of a Bureau of Land Management boat launch and campground, another popular fishing hole. Continue another mile to a point where Highway 3 approaches the trail and a private camping area sits on the riverbank. Just beyond, at **3.8** miles, is the Lane Wayside, your turnaround spot.

Going Farther

It's 1.7 miles from Lane to the Black Rock Trailhead, where Highway 3 crosses the Coeur d'Alene River, making a round-trip hike of 11.0 miles. ∎

51. Trail of the Coeur d'Alenes, Bull Run–Black Rock

RATING	DISTANCE	HIKING TIME
★★☆☆☆	5.2 miles round-trip	2.5 hours

ELEVATION GAIN	HIGH POINT	DIFFICULTY
20 feet	2,130 feet	◆◇◇◇◇

BEST MONTHS
Jan Feb **Mar Apr May Jun Jul Aug Sep Oct** Nov Dec

The Hike

The whole family can enjoy this river walk through portions of the Coeur d'Alene River Wildlife Management Area.

Getting There

Follow Interstate 90 east from Coeur d'Alene to exit 34 for State Route 3. Follow Highway 3 southwest for 3.4 miles to South Bull Run Road in the community of Rose Lake and turn left across the bridge. Turn right just across the bridge and follow South Bull Run a quarter-mile to the trailhead and parking area on the right, 2,130 feet above sea level. Restrooms and a picnic area are located here.

The Trail

This is the shortest section of the Trail of the Coeur d'Alenes that stays on the side of the river away from main roads, yielding more

---

PERMITS/CONTACT
None required/Idaho Department of Parks and Recreation, (208) 682-3814, www.parksandrecreation.idaho.gov

MAPS
USGS Rose Lake, USGS Lane; Trail of the Coeur d'Alenes map

TRAIL NOTES
Leashed dogs OK; bikes welcome

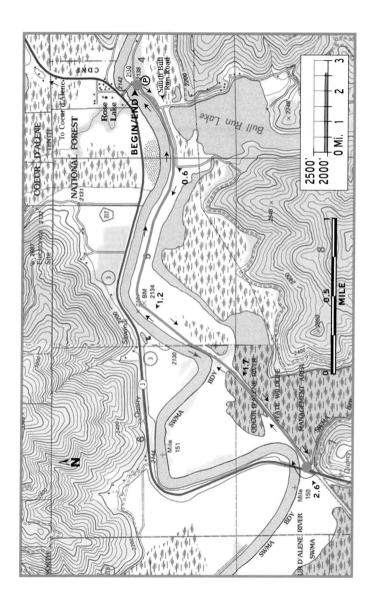

Colorful fields along the trail

opportunities for spotting wildlife and enjoying a walk away from traffic noise. This is a good walk to take in the morning with the sun at your back.

Begin by following the river downstream to the east on a causeway separating it from Bull Run Lake to the south. The lake looks as if you could walk across it on water lilies during the summer and is frequently visited by great blue herons. Beyond the lake at **0.6** mile, follow the river as it bends to the south and passes an old sawmill on the other side of the river, **1.2** miles from the trailhead.

To continue, the trail leaves the river and crosses a wide marsh, a prime area for waterfowl and moose, as well as a "bale" of turtles we spotted occupying a log in the marsh at **1.7** miles. B. B. Hardbody called them the more common "herd" and squirted her water bottle at me when I corrected her.

You'll reach the Black Rock parking area underneath the Highway 3 bridge at **2.6** miles, your turnaround spot. The river here is a popular swimming hole with local youngsters.

Going Farther

You can continue another 1.4 miles one-way to the Lane Wayside, making a round-trip hike of 8 miles. ■

52. Trail of the Coeur d'Alenes, Bull Run–River Bend

RATING	DISTANCE	HIKING TIME
★ ★ ★ ★ ☆	10.0 miles round-trip	5.5 hours

ELEVATION GAIN	HIGH POINT	DIFFICULTY
20 feet	2,140 feet	♦ ♦ ◇ ◇ ◇

BEST MONTHS
Jan Feb **Mar Apr May Jun Jul Aug Sep Oct** Nov Dec

The Hike

This is the best way to see the beautiful Coeur d'Alene River: slowly on foot along quiet waters amidst evergreen forests and emerald meadows.

Getting There

Follow Interstate 90 east from Coeur d'Alene to exit 34 for State Route 3. Follow Highway 3 southwest for 3.4 miles to South Bull Run Road in the community of Rose Lake and turn left across the bridge. Turn right just across the bridge and follow South Bull Run a quarter-mile to the trailhead and parking area on the right, 2,130 feet above sea level. Restrooms and a picnic area are located here.

PERMITS/CONTACT
None required/Idaho Department of Parks and Recreation,
(208) 682-3814, www.parksandrecreation.idaho.gov

MAPS
USGS Rose Lake; Trail of the Coeur d'Alenes map

TRAIL NOTES
Leashed dogs OK; bikes welcome

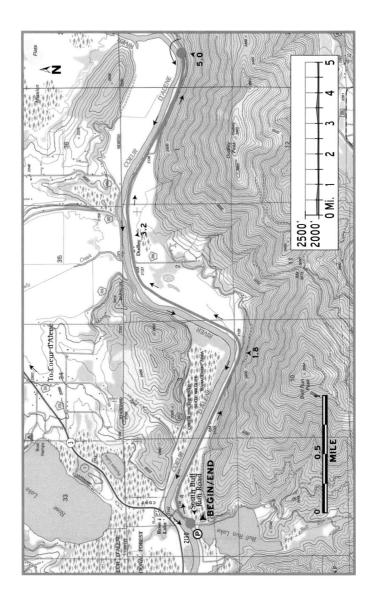

The Trail

The section of the Trail of the Coeur d'Alenes from Bull Run to the River Bend Wayside makes a good late-afternoon or evening walk, when you're more apt to spot wildlife and expend pixels getting selfies with moose in the background. The light will be at your back on the way out, so when you turn to face your phone, you'll be high-lighted along with the moose behind you. (Note: If the moose's ears are laid back and it is making grunting noises at you, the wise thing to do is forget the selfie and get the hell out of there.)

Walk around a bend in the river and head southeast along the shoreline, which grows increasingly close to the forested slopes of 3,994-foot-high Bull Run Peak on your right. This shady section of trail leads, in 1.8 miles, to a wide green meadow where the path turns to the northeast and tree-covered slopes across the river stretch steeply 600 vertical feet. When hiking this section on a hot summer day in 2016, we found a "trail angel"—as Pacific Crest Trail thru-hikers call folks who help them along the way—offering drinking water to passersby.

You'll walk another 1.4 miles along the meadow to the Dudley Wayside, where you'll find a picnic table and a good turnaround spot for families with younger hikers, **3.2** miles from the trailhead. From here, the path makes a wide bend to the south and enters another area shaded by forest on the slopes of Dudley Peak to the south. At **5.0** miles, you'll reach a bend in the river called (spoiler alert) River Bend. This is a good turnaround spot, with picnic tables and a restroom.

Going Farther

You can walk another 3.5 miles to the Cataldo Trailhead off I-90, which would make a long round-trip of 16 miles. Another option for hikers with two cars would be to walk one-way between Bull Run and Cataldo. ∎

53. Trail of the Coeur d'Alenes, Cataldo–River Bend

RATING	DISTANCE	HIKING TIME
★★☆☆☆	**8.0 miles round-trip**	**4 hours**

ELEVATION GAIN	HIGH POINT	DIFFICULTY
20 feet	**2,130 feet**	◆◇◇◇◇

BEST MONTHS
~~Jan~~ ~~Feb~~ **Mar** **Apr** **May** ~~Jun~~ ~~Jul~~ ~~Aug~~ **Sep** **Oct** ~~Nov~~ ~~Dec~~

The Hike

Here's a river walk that will give you a lesson in history while getting a good spring tune-up or fall workout.

Getting There

Drive east on Interstate 90 from Coeur d'Alene to exit 40. Turn right onto South Latour Creek Road and drive 0.2 mile to the parking area and trailhead on the left, 2,130 feet above sea level. There are no public restrooms.

The Trail

It takes about a mile of walking to drown out the incessant rumble of the highway as you walk southwest and pass under I-90. A campground on your right attracts interstate travelers, kayakers, and hikers. The way is across open fields for 1.5 miles to Old Mission

---

PERMITS/CONTACT
None required/Idaho Department of Parks and Recreation,
(208) 682-3814, www.parksandrecreation.idaho.gov

MAPS
USGS Cataldo, USGS Rose Lake; Trail of the Coeur d'Alenes map

TRAIL NOTES
Leashed dogs OK; bikes welcome

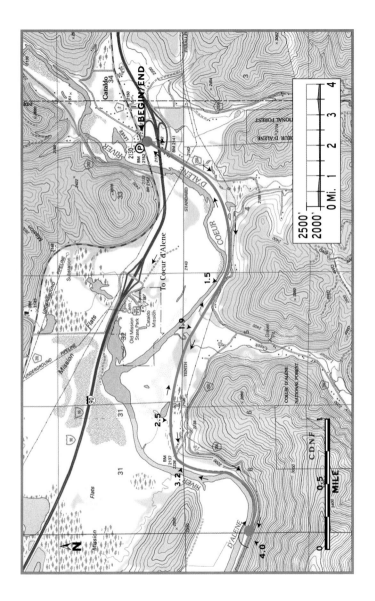

La Tour Creek

viewpoint with its picnic table. Look across the river to Old Mission State Park and the Mission of the Sacred Heart, the oldest building in Idaho. Construction began in 1850 and took three years to complete. The mission grounds and park are popular spots for family gatherings and weddings.

Farther along, you'll cross Latour Creek at **1.9** miles, which interpretive signs tell you is a good place to catch trout and mountain whitefish. Cross river flats for another half-mile to a pond and wetland before a sweeping bend in the route, at **3.2** miles, takes you south along the riverside, shaded by evergreens of the Coeur d'Alene National Forest.

Walk another 0.8 mile to the River Bend Wayside, where you'll find restrooms and picnic tables. This pretty spot by the river is your turn-around spot.

Going Farther

It's another 2.2 miles to the Dudley Wayside, where a picnic table is located. That would make the round-trip hike from Cataldo 12.4 miles, a long walk even on a paved, level surface. ■

54. Trail of the Coeur d'Alenes, Cataldo–Enaville

RATING	DISTANCE	HIKING TIME
★ ★ ★ ★ ★	10.0 miles round-trip	5.5 hours
ELEVATION GAIN	**HIGH POINT**	**DIFFICULTY**
40 feet	2,170 feet	◆ ◆ ◇ ◇ ◇
	BEST MONTHS	
Jan Feb Mar **Apr May Jun Jul Aug Sep Oct** Nov Dec		

The Hike

If you've got time for only one hike along the Trail of the Coeur d'Alenes, make it this one.

Getting There

Drive east on Interstate 90 from Coeur d'Alene to exit 40. Turn right onto South Latour Creek Road and drive 0.2 mile to the parking area and trailhead on the left, 2,130 feet above sea level. There are no public restrooms.

PERMITS/CONTACT
None required/Idaho Department of Parks and Recreation,
(208) 682-3814, www.parksandrecreation.idaho.gov

MAPS
USGS Cataldo, USGS Kellogg West; Trail of the Coeur d'Alenes map

TRAIL NOTES
Leashed dogs OK; bikes welcome

The view downriver at the River Bend rest stop

The Trail

Two reasons make this the best hike on the Trail of the Coeur d'Alenes.

- You are never near a major highway or road, surrounded only by forest and bounded by river, where you'll find spots for picnicking, swimming, or fishing, except at the trailheads.

- The Enaville trailhead is just a stomach's growl away from some of the best grub and beverages in the Idaho Panhandle at the Snake Pit. You needn't pack a lunch on this hike—but don't overdo it since you've got to walk 5 miles back to your car.

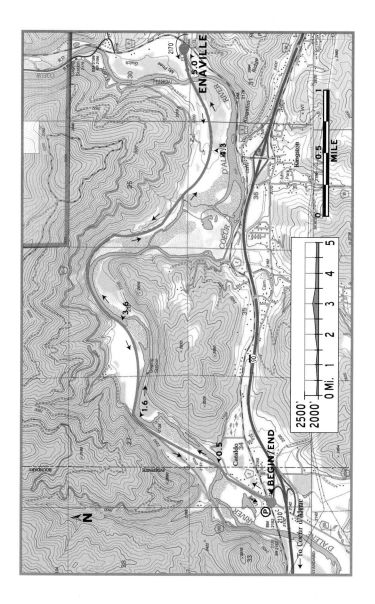

Begin by walking northeast through the community of Cataldo and crossing the old railroad bridge at **0.5** mile. Leave the racket of I-90 behind as you stroll upriver and quickly duck behind a 2,650-foot-high forested hill to the south that isolates the trail from the highway. A country road parallels the path for a mile or so but rarely sees any traffic. At **1.6** miles, arrive at Pine Meadows, the first of three great picnic spots on the way to Enaville.

Gap Rock, the second, is another 0.7 mile up the trail. The river is deep here and an excellent swimming hole during the hot summer months. Walk under cliffs just above the trail and turn south to the Backwater Bay Wayside, **3.6** miles from the trailhead. The broad beaches host waterfowl nesting sites, and anglers often float the main stem of the river to the south.

The trail now crosses a flat plateau away from the river with farmland to the north and mature pine forest between you and the water at **4.3** miles. In about a half-mile, you'll arrive at a bridge just upstream of the confluence of the north and south forks of the Coeur d'Alene River. Walk another quarter-mile to the Enaville Trailhead, where you'll find picnic tables, a restroom, and just across the road, the Snake Pit.

Going Farther

Another 1.7 one-way miles of the Trail of the Coeur d'Alenes follows the south fork of the river away from major roads, and is an excellent way to get a few more miles. The trail leads to the Pine Creek Trailhead, with picnic tables, restrooms, and a mile-long connector route to the community of Pinehurst. ■

55. Trail of the Coeur d'Alenes, Pine Creek–Gap Rock

RATING	DISTANCE	HIKING TIME
★★★ ☆☆	8.8 miles round-trip	4.5 hours

ELEVATION GAIN	HIGH POINT	DIFFICULTY
30 feet	2,175 feet	◆ ◇ ◇ ◇ ◇

BEST MONTHS
Jan Feb **Mar Apr May** Jun Jul Aug **Sep Oct** Nov Dec

The Hike

Walk a quiet section of the Trail of the Coeur d'Alenes and—it's probably still there—see a bike in a tree.

Getting There

Drive east on Interstate 90 from Coeur d'Alene to exit 45 for Pinehurst. Turn left on North Division Street (Old Highway 10) and go under the interstate. Turn left about 450 feet past the on-ramp, and drive downhill to the parking area and trailhead, 2,175 feet above sea level. A restroom and picnic tables are located here.

The Trail

The first nearly 2 miles of this walk are sheltered from highway noise by 2,700-foot-high Kingston Ridge to the south. The south fork of

---

PERMITS/CONTACT
None required/Idaho Department of Parks and Recreation,
(208) 682-3814, www.parksandrecreation.idaho.gov

MAPS
USGS Cataldo, USGS Kellogg West; Trail of the Coeur d'Alenes map

TRAIL NOTES
Leashed dogs OK; bikes welcome

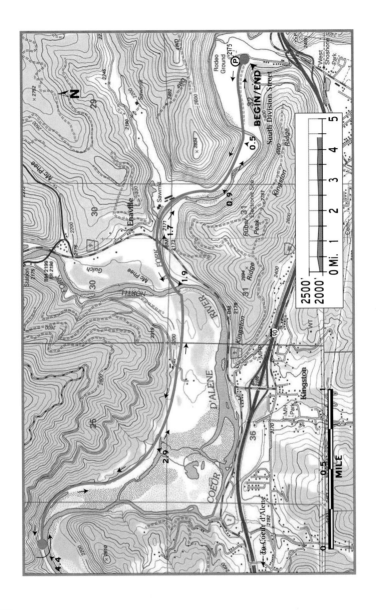

The bicycle in the tree near Enaville

the Coeur d'Alene River ripples clear along its gravel bed, and local anglers enjoy easy access to the water from the trailhead.

The route heads west and crosses the river on the old railroad bridge, **0.5** mile from the trailhead. The path then turns away from the water, which takes a big bend to the south, and follows the forested edge of McLeod Hill. River flats on the left are sparsely vegetated, which makes for good walking off pavement when the river is low. At **0.9** mile, look to the right about 40 feet off the trail in a thick grove of aspens. We're betting you'll see the same thing we saw: a bicycle hanging about halfway up a tree.

We met a couple of local hikers who told us it had been there for at least four years and that nobody was certain who put it there. It looked like a nice bike too—far nicer than the bicycle I ride, The Great Emasculator.

Continuing west, the trail passes a rock quarry and old sawmill before crossing Forest Highway 9 at **1.7** miles. This splendid road follows the beautiful north fork of the Coeur d'Alene River for miles upstream, passing popular Coeur d'Alene National Forest campgrounds. Up the road to the right is the Snake Pit, a favorite watering hole of locals and tourists alike for decades.

Cross the road to the Enaville Trailhead, with picnic tables and a restroom. At **1.9** miles, walk the bridge over the Coeur d'Alene River just upstream from its fork. The route curves west across a wide meadow for a mile to the Backwater Bay Wayside at **2.9** miles. The gravel river flats here provide excellent nesting grounds for waterfowl.

The path now turns in a wide bend, and forested ridges rise more than 3,800 feet to the north. To the south, the evergreen hills create a barrier to both interstate noise and civilization. The route narrows under cliffs and rounds a bend at Gap Rock Wayside, **4.4** miles from the trailhead and your turnaround spot. The picnic tables here are ideally located above one of the best swimming holes on the river.

Going Farther

Combine this walk with the Cataldo–Enaville trail (Hike 54). That would add 3.4 miles round-trip for a 13.4-mile hike along the very best hiking the Trail of the Coeur d'Alenes has to offer. Parties with two cars can make a 6.7-mile one-way hike by leaving one car at Pine Creek and the other at Cataldo. ■

COEUR D'ALENE NORTHEAST

56. English Point Loops

RATING	DISTANCE	HIKING TIME
★★☆☆☆	5.0 miles round-trip	2.5 hours
ELEVATION GAIN	**HIGH POINT**	**DIFFICULTY**
320 feet	2,570 feet	◆◆◇◇◇

BEST MONTHS
Jan Feb Mar **Apr May Jun** Jul Aug **Sep Oct** Nov Dec

The Hike
This woodsy walk is a good spring workout and a trek for the entire family.

Getting There
Take exit 12 from Interstate 90 in Coeur d'Alene and drive north on US Route 95 for 6 miles to Lancaster Road and turn right. Drive 3.5 miles to English Point Road and turn right. The parking area and trailhead are on the immediate left, 2,570 feet above sea level. A restroom is available.

The Trail
English Point is a parcel of the Idaho Panhandle National Forest that makes an excellent getaway from the surrounding suburban areas. You'll have company here pretty much any time of the year, and it's a good cross-country skiing and snowshoeing area during winter

---

PERMITS/CONTACT
None required/Idaho Panhandle National Forest, Coeur d'Alene River Ranger District, (208) 664-2318, www.fs.usda.gov/ipnf

MAPS
USGS Hayden Lake; kiosk map

TRAIL NOTES
Leashed dogs OK; bikes and equestrians welcome (some on separate trails)

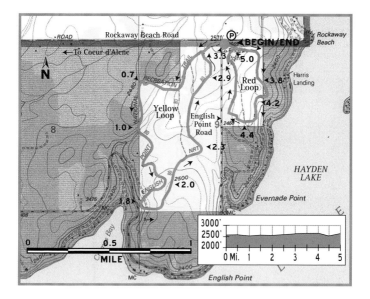

months when there's adequate snow. Families with young children like the trail signs that are color coded and keep the kids on track.

The route recommended here combines two of the longer hikes, the Yellow Loop, which begins across English Point Road from the trailhead, and the Red Loop, which starts at a gate in the parking lot. To begin, cross the road to the Yellow Loop and hike southwest, keeping to the right at junctions with the Blue Loop and turning right at the Green Loop. At **0.7** mile, you arrive at a fence line marking the forest boundary and turn along the fence, staying right at the next trail junction, **1.0** mile from the trailhead.

The path reenters a sparse pine forest and crosses several boardwalks over areas that may be soggy in the spring. At **1.8** miles, turn east above Hayden Bluff Lane, where you get a tree-ka-boo view of Cramps Bay on Hayden Lake. The route now turns north toward the trailhead, passing a clearing at **2.0** miles and reaching a trail junction with the Green Trail at **2.3** miles. Turn right at the junction and pass benches in the pine forest above English

The trailhead

Point Road. At **2.9** miles, stay right at the junction with the Blue Loop and 0.3 mile later, turn right to close the loop, arriving at the trailhead after **3.3** miles.

Recross the English Point Road and begin the Red Loop hike at the north end of the parking area. The path parallels Lancaster Road for about 0.5 mile to a junction with the Gray Loop at **3.8** miles. Stay left and continue to tree-obscured views of Hayden Lake at **4.2** miles and then **4.4** miles, where you'll find an observation platform. The trail now turns west and climbs back to parallel English Point Road, arriving back at the trailhead for a total of **5.0** miles.

Going Farther

You can combine several shorter loops on both sides of English Point Road to get a total hike of 8.2 miles. ■

57. Fourth of July Loop

RATING	DISTANCE	HIKING TIME
★★★☆☆	5.4 miles round-trip	2.5 hours

ELEVATION GAIN	HIGH POINT	DIFFICULTY
240 feet	3,280 feet	◆◆◆◆◆

BEST MONTHS
Jan Feb Mar Apr May **Jun Jul Aug Sep Oct** Nov Dec

The Hike
This is a pleasant family walk through evergreen forests both old and young with a good chance of spotting wildlife.

Getting There
Drive east on Interstate 90 from Coeur d'Alene to the summit of Fourth of July Pass at exit 28, and turn right on the paved and gravel road leading west above the highway. Drive 0.3 mile, staying right on the lower road at a Y junction, to the parking area and trailhead, 3,090 feet above sea level. A restroom is available.

The Trail
Hikers can thank the Idaho Panhandle National Forest and the good folk of the Panhandle Nordic Club for the opportunity to trek so close to Coeur d'Alene and Spokane. The trails—mostly old logging roads—are extremely well marked so cross-country skiers and snowshoe hikers

PERMITS/CONTACT
None (Park N' Ski pass required in winter)/Idaho Panhandle National Forest, (208) 664-2318, www.fs.usda.gov/ipnf; Panhandle Nordic Club, www.panhandlenordicclub.com

MAPS
USGS Lane; PDF trail map at www.panhandlenordicclub.com

TRAIL NOTES
Leashed dogs OK; bikes welcome

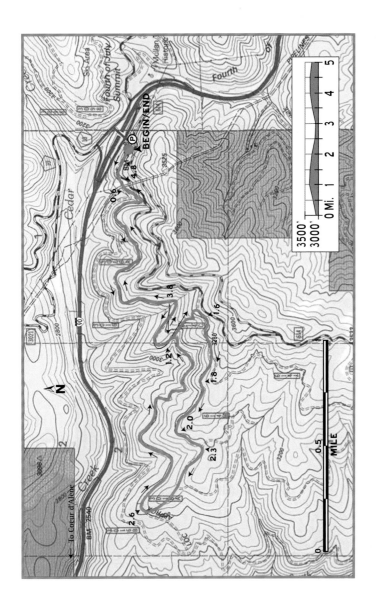

won't lose their way in the winter, and these same trail markers will keep all the no-snow hoofers on the right track as well.

Loop hikes vary in distance, and the inner loop hike suggested here represents a compromise between shorter and longer treks that can be found. Begin at the gated road at the west end of

Panhandle Hut

the parking lot and follow the wide path into timber, traversing the hillside for 0.6 mile to the Panhandle Hut, a nice little A-frame that serves as a warming hut for cross-country skiers and snowshoe hikers.

Past the hut and groomer shed, the route climbs very gently to a trail junction that shouldn't be hard to miss because you'll see a sign that reads "The Junction," **1.2** miles from the trailhead. Turn left here onto the Loose Moose Trail. Despite the name, you are just as likely to see moose on any other trail on this hike.

At **1.6** miles, Loose Moose meets Skate Away Trail, where you'll stay right and emerge onto the High Road Trail. In another 0.2 mile, you'll get a good view to the west, courtesy of an Idaho Panhandle National Forest white pine restoration project. Beyond, the route meets Spencer's S Trail, **2.0** miles from the trailhead. Stay right and continue to a picnic shelter and restroom at **2.3** miles at a junction with High Road and the Swoop Trail.

In another 0.1 mile, turn right at a black diamond trail named White Knuckles. As a backcountry skier whose sitzmarker is callused from overuse, I can tell you the name is appropriate. Walk down the steep hillside to the west to a trail junction with Havin' Fun at **2.6** miles and turn right. You'll be hiking along the lower section of the restoration project for 1.2 miles and climbing back up to The Junction at **3.8** miles. Pass the warming hut at **4.8** miles, arriving at the parking area after another 0.6 mile.

Going Farther

You can add almost 4 miles to your hike by turning left at the picnic shelter and following the Elderberry Trail, Eagle Run, Skywalker, and Twisted Klister (Forest Road 614) side routes on your way back to the trailhead. ■

58. Coal Creek

RATING	DISTANCE	HIKING TIME
★★☆☆☆	9.6 miles round-trip	5.5 hours

ELEVATION GAIN	HIGH POINT	DIFFICULTY
3,460 feet	5,727 feet	◆◆◆◆◆

BEST MONTHS		
Jan Feb Mar Apr May **Jun Jul Aug Sep** Oct Nov Dec		

The Hike

Save this steep, long climb for an early August day, when huckleberries are the reward near the summit of Graham Mountain.

Getting There

Drive east on Interstate 90 from Coeur d'Alene to exit 43 for Kingston, and turn north on Forest Highway 9, the scenic highway up the north fork of the Coeur d'Alene River with its many campgrounds. Drive 13.1 miles to a signed junction on the right and turn right, driving less than 0.1 mile up a dirt road to the trailhead, 2,320 feet above sea level.

The Trail

The Coal Creek Trail No. 41 was our first real physical test when we hiked it in August 2016—one I failed with flying colors. Only the ripe huckleberries we found in the shaded high timber below Graham Mountain saved me from collapsing like a detumescent slug in the middle of the path, never to humidify again.

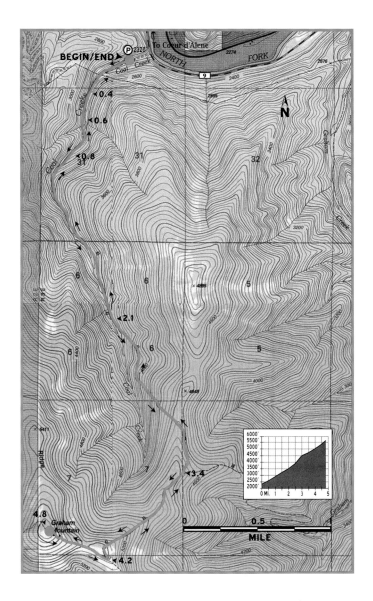

BEGIN/END

To Coeur d'Alene

NORTH FORK

2320

Coal Creek

<0.4

<0.6

<0.8

31

31

32

6

6

6

6

4.8

Graham Mountain

<4.2

<2.1

<3.4

5

5

Ridge

Coal Creek

Graham Creek

N

MILE

0   0.5

6000'
5500'
5000'
4500'
4000'
3500'
3000'
2500'
2000'
0 Mi.   1   2   3   4   5

A timber bridge crosses Coal Creek

The first part of this climb isn't all that bad. Walk past a couple of diverse campsites and climb along Coal Creek, in the timber to your left. The raison d'être for this trail becomes clear at **0.4** mile, when you pass an old mine shaft in the hill above the trail. At **0.6** mile, cross Coal Creek on a bridge and climb another 0.8 mile to a rock ledge and a mining claim declaring the rock belongs to the Coal Creek Mining Company.

You'll continue climbing along a sidehill traverse, passing open slopes covered with paintbrush and pearly everlasting. Reach the only easy access to Coal Creek at **2.1** miles, your water source for the rest of the hike. (Note: After huckleberries revived me and I was able to waddle down the trail, I did not rush back in the autumn to see if Coal Creek ran dry. I hope you will forgive.)

PERMITS/CONTACT
None required/Idaho Panhandle National Forest,
(208) 783-2363, www.fs.usda.gov/ipnf

MAPS
USGS Kellogg East, USGS Kellogg West, USGS Grizzly Mountain, USGS
Steamboat Creek; PDF trail at www.fs.usda.gov/ipnf

TRAIL NOTES
Leashed dogs OK

The climbing really gets steep at this point, as Coal Creek tumbles through an ever-narrowing gorge and you climb 1,000 vertical feet in about 0.7 mile. At **3.4** miles, near the end of the climb, reach a junction with Graham Creek Trail No. 33. Stay right and find a section of the path that actually goes downhill—at least for several hundred yards.

Beyond, at **4.2** miles, reach a junction with Graham Ridge Trail No. 17. Turn right over a 5,400-foot saddle and alpine meadow and climb to the summit of Graham Mountain, 5,727 feet above sea level. Here is your spot to turn around, or in my case, collapse in a sweaty heap. Consume huckleberries.

Going Farther

I can't imagine anyone wanting to go farther. But if by chance you are an Olympic athlete, a trail marathoner, or the guy who in 2016 climbed up and down Mount Rainier in 4 hours and 24 minutes, you can walk back via the Graham Ridge and Graham Creek Trails, which end on Forest Highway 9 about 1.7 miles northeast of the Coal Creek Trailhead. The total distance would be about 14 miles. ∎

59. Pulaski Trail

RATING	DISTANCE	HIKING TIME
★★★★☆	4.0 miles round-trip	3 hours

ELEVATION GAIN	HIGH POINT	DIFFICULTY
950 feet	3,890 feet	◆◆◆◇◇

BEST MONTHS
Jan Feb Mar Apr **May Jun Jul Aug Sep** Oct Nov Dec

The Hike

Don't miss this family climb through time to the 1910 wildfire that destroyed more than 3 million acres of forest, and meet the man who saved the lives of thirty-seven firefighters.

Getting There

Drive east on Interstate 90 from Coeur d'Alene for about 49 miles to exit 61 for Wallace. Turn right on North Frontage Road and follow it one block to Front Street and turn left. Follow Front to 2nd Street and turn right. Follow 2nd to Bank Street and turn right, following Bank as it turns left and becomes King Street. Follow King, renamed Placer Creek Road (Forest Road 456), uphill for about 0.8 mile to the parking area and trailhead, 2,960 feet above sea level. Restrooms are available and the path begins across the road. The first 725 feet are wheelchair accessible.

PERMITS/CONTACT
None required/Idaho Panhandle National Forest,
(208) 783-2363, www.fs.usda.gov/ipnf

MAPS
USGS Wallace; kiosk map

TRAIL NOTES
Leashed dogs OK

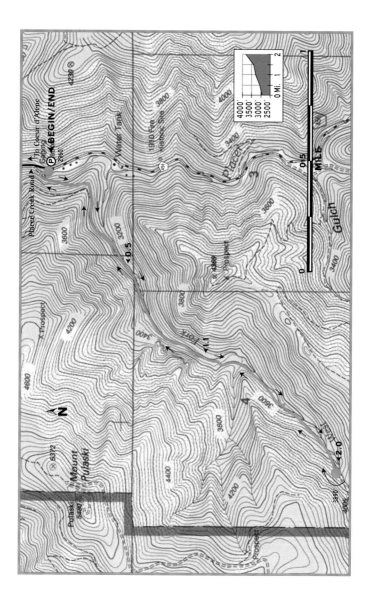

The Trail

Though this might be considered a long drive for such a short trek, especially for Spokane hikers, don't pass up the chance to hike the Pulaski Trail if you've the time. With every step, you'll retrace the steps of forty-three men who followed Ed Pulaski to a haven from a giant killer fire. Pulaski, a ranger who led his crew as Wallace burned during the "Big Blow" of August 1910, raced the fire to the Nicholson Mine, where the men took shelter. Six firefighters in Pulaski's crew perished and eighty-five people were killed in the massive blaze.

Besides his heroism, Ed Pulaski is remembered as the inventor of the tool that bears his name. Trail crews and firefighters throughout American forests use the Pulaski, a combined ax and adze. In a genius stroke, Idaho Panhandle National Forest planners decorated the many interpretive signs along the trail with Pulaski tools.

Give yourself plenty of time on the path to read all of the interpretive signs along the way, which describe everything from mining techniques to quotes from Pulaski's descriptions of the fire. A memorial to the firefighters can be found at the Pulaski Tunnel at your turnaround point, 2 miles from the trailhead.

After crossing Placer Creek, the route turns west and the paved portion ends. The path climbs steadily on a moderate grade, with short, steep sections that take the hiker farther away from the west fork of Placer Creek below. At **1.1** miles, find a sign describing a "Buffalo Blower," a water-driven ventilator for a mine in this silver-rich country.

The route beyond climbs away from the creek to cross a tributary stream, passing a huge old cedar snag still standing from the 1910 fire. The last 0.5 mile to the memorial is the steepest, and very steep way trails lead down to cross the creek to the Pulaski Tunnel. An interpretive sign at the memorial explains that the tunnel entrance is a restoration by Wallace artist Hal Payne.

Going Farther

The Pulaski Trail continues up the west fork of Placer Creek for another mile, crossing the creek and joining a trail that climbs up from Cranky Gulch, to the south. ■

60. Marie Creek

RATING	DISTANCE	HIKING TIME
★★★ ☆ ☆	8.2 miles round-trip	4.5 hours

ELEVATION GAIN	HIGH POINT	DIFFICULTY
1,220 feet	2,800 feet	♦ ♦ ♦ ◇ ◇

BEST MONTHS
Jan Feb Mar Apr **May Jun Jul Aug Sep Oct** Nov Dec

The Hike

Here's a pleasant walk through forest and meadow along a clear mountain stream, where soggy trails linger long into summer.

Getting There

Drive east on Interstate 90 from Coeur d'Alene for 10 miles to exit 22 for State Route 97. Go north and drive over the I-90 overpass. Turn right on the frontage road, Forest Road 119, and drive 1 mile to Wolf Lodge Road (FR 202). Turn left and drive to Wolf Lodge in 1.8 miles, bearing left on FR 202 at Wolf Lodge for 1.8 miles to a junction with FR 1581. Turn right and continue on FR 202 for 1.1 miles to the trailhead parking area down a dirt road on the right.

The Trail

The Marie Creek Trail is popular with equestrians and backpackers looking to find a quiet spot to camp in meadows beside the creek. The lowlands and trail can get pretty soggy in the early season and we

PERMITS/CONTACT
None required/Idaho Panhandle National Forest,
(208) 783-2363, www.fs.usda.gov/ipnf

MAPS
USGS Wolf Lodge; PDF trail map at www.fs.usda.gov/ipnf

TRAIL NOTES
Leashed dogs OK; equestrians welcome

61. Farragut State Park, Beaver–Buttonhook Bay Loops

RATING	DISTANCE	HIKING TIME
★★★★☆	6.8 miles round-trip	3.5 hours
ELEVATION GAIN	**HIGH POINT**	**DIFFICULTY**
580 feet	2,400 feet	◆◆◇◇◇
BEST MONTHS		
Jan Feb Mar Apr May **Jun Jul Aug Sep** Oct Nov Dec		

The Hike
Expect plenty of company on this waterfront walk along the biggest—and many say most beautiful—lake in the Inland Northwest.

Getting There
Take exit 12 from Interstate 90 and turn north on US Route 95 for a little more than 18 miles to Athol. Turn right on State Route 54 and drive 4.5 miles to the Farragut State Park Visitor Center on the right, where you can purchase a day-use pass ($5 in 2017) and get trail information and a map handout. To continue, turn right on South Road and drive 3.3 miles to the Willow Day Use Area and trailhead, 2,070 feet above sea level, where restrooms are available.

Spokane hikers wishing to avoid traffic in Coeur d'Alene and Hayden can take exit 7 from I-90 east of Post Falls and drive north on State Route 41 to Boekel Road. Turn right and follow Boekel to

PERMITS/CONTACT
Day-use pass required/Farragut State Park, (208) 683-2425, www.parksandrecreation.idaho.gov

MAPS
USGS Bayview; Farragut PDF, handout maps

TRAIL NOTES
Leashed dogs OK; bikes welcome

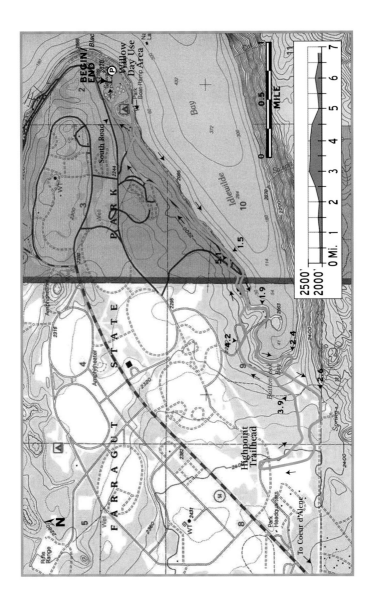

its junction with US 95 north of Hayden, then continue with the directions on page 218.

The Trail

Farragut State Park, once a Naval Training Center and later the site for several national and world Scout jamborees, is now an extremely popular camping, boating, mountain biking, hiking, and fishing destination for outdoorsfolk throughout the Northwest and beyond. Hundreds of campsites are available by reservation only and are full throughout the summer months. The 4,000-acre park serves up a confusing jumble of hiking trails that can keep a day hiker busy for weeks, but the lakeshore loop here is arguably the nicest walk in the park.

First, a few words about Farragut trails: once you catch the numbering method, you're on your way. The top number indicates the trail junction you are at, not the trail number. The numbers below with arrows show the direction to that junction. We scratched our heads and wondered why they didn't simply number the trails.

Find the Lakeview Trail at the south end of the parking area and drop down to the path along the shoreline. Head southwest along the shore, then either follow the paved road across the Eagle Boat Launch or take trails up and around the boat launch. Both routes merge on the boat launch road, which you cross, and return to the shoreline.

Walk along the shoreline for 1.5 miles and come to a big parking area at the Beaver Bay beach. At the southwest end of the parking area, find a trail that circles the bay and swimming beach and turns south. This path joins a shoreline route at Buttonhook Bay at **1.9** miles, before it leaves the shoreline and climbs to a couple of viewpoints **2.4** miles from the trailhead.

The path continues to climb to a mess of trail junctions that all lead westerly toward the park visitor center and southeast to Bernard Peak and the Scout Trail. We followed a path to the Highpoint Trail and turned right at **2.6** miles, hiking to the Highpoint Trailhead. From there, we turned right and followed the other end of the Highpoint Trail as it looped north, then east to Junction 50 at **3.9** miles. This short path connects to the Squirrel Cache Loop, where you'll turn

The trail along Lake Pend Oreille

right and follow it past a kiosk regaling the steamboat *Mary Moody*, **4.2** miles from the trailhead.

Just beyond, follow the trail and road to the Buttonhook Group Camp and stay right to Junction 57, which drops to the right at Beaver Bay beach. Follow the shore back to the big parking lot and stay left on the upper Beaver Bay Shoreline Loop Trail. This wide path is a shady return above the shoreline, **5.1** miles from the trailhead. You can follow it back to the Eagle Boat Launch and trailhead or take the path along the shoreline for a 6.3-mile hike.

Going Farther

This route can be combined with any number of trails in the park. Perhaps the most rewarding would be the climb to the Highpoint viewpoint, which would add about 2.6 miles to the hike. The Scout Trail is a rugged 17-mile round-trip climb to Bernard Peak. The park campgrounds make excellent base camps for exploring the trails, but reservations must be made months in advance. ■

62. Farragut State Park, Willow Lakeview–Buggy Trail Loops

RATING	DISTANCE	HIKING TIME
★★☆☆☆	7.0 miles round-trip	4 hours

ELEVATION GAIN	HIGH POINT	DIFFICULTY
260 feet	2,300 feet	◆◆◇◇◇

BEST MONTHS
Jan Feb Mar Apr **May Jun Jul Aug Sep** Oct Nov Dec

The Hike

This trek begins and ends with the opportunity to take a swim in the cold, cold waters of Lake Pend Oreille.

Getting There

Take exit 12 from Interstate 90 and turn north on US Route 95 for a little more than 18 miles to Athol. Turn right on State Route 54 and drive 4.5 miles to the Farragut State Park Visitor Center on the right, where you can purchase a day-use pass ($5 in 2016) and get trail information and a map handout. To continue, turn right on South Road and drive 3.3 miles to the Willow Day Use Area and trailhead, 2,070 feet above sea level, where restrooms are available.

Spokane hikers wishing to avoid traffic in Coeur d'Alene and Hayden can take exit 7 from I-90 east of Post Falls and drive north

---

PERMITS/CONTACT
Day-use pass required/Farragut State Park,
(208) 683-2425, www.parksandrecreation.idaho.gov

MAPS
USGS Bayview; Farragut PDF, handout maps

TRAIL NOTES
Leashed dogs OK; bikes welcome; equestrians and llamas welcome
north of State Route 54

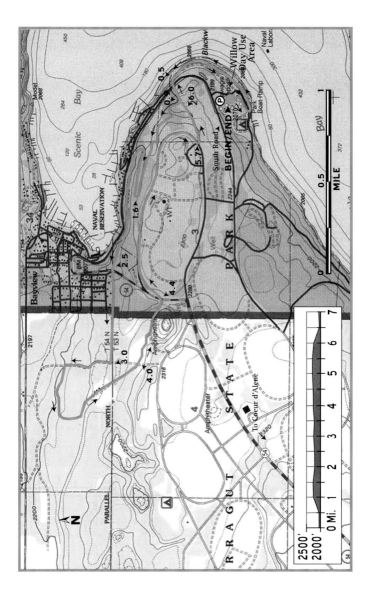

on State Route 41 to Boekel Road. Turn right and follow Boekel to its junction with US 95 north of Hayden, then continue with the directions on page 222.

The Trail

Farragut State Park's trails are best suited for hikers who are seeking exercise in a forest environment where seeing wildlife or enjoying mountain scenery might not be a top priority. The lake itself and surrounding mountains are beautiful, no question. And wildlife such as white-tailed deer, moose, and black bear are often seen. But even with 4,000 acres of Navy training facilities and 45 miles of trails slowly returning to nature, it is not a place where you'll find the solitude and beauty of a spot—as the Wilderness Act specifies—that is untrammeled by man.

The walk recommended here begins and ends on the Willow Lakeview Loop Trail, where you'll find ample opportunity for a hike-ending swim. Take the trail at the south end of the parking area down to the shoreline and Junction 74. (For reasons beyond our ken, trail junctions—not trails—are numbered. The top number on the post is the junction you are at and the numbers below with arrows show the direction of the next junction.)

Turn left at Junction 74 and follow it along the shoreline for 0.4 mile to a bluff and sign identifying this as a former Navy firing range. In another 0.1 mile, stay right at Junction 84 and follow the trail past 85 to 86, **0.9** mile from the trailhead, where you'll turn right, walking in moss-carpeted forest to Junction 91 at **1.6** miles. Turn right, here, and follow the trail as it switches back down toward Hudson Bay Road and Scenic Bay to the outskirts of Bayview.

At **2.5** miles, cross SR 54 and follow the park boundary past a number of Bayview cabins. Continue past Junction 17 to 16, **3.0** miles from the trailhead, and turn right on the Buggy Trail. Follow this a short distance downhill to Junction 15 and turn left. The route passes Junction 25 and turns east, recrossing the Buggy Trail at **4.0** miles.

Now walk past the amphitheater, passing Junctions 23 and 21 and recrossing Highway 54 at **4.4** miles. Turn left at Junction 93 and walk downhill to an abandoned road. Turn right on the road and follow it past Junctions 92 and 90 to the Locust Grove Group Camp, **5.7** miles from the trailhead. Turn left at Junction 89 and follow it downhill past 88 to 86, where you'll close the loop at **6.0** miles. Drop down to the shoreline and turn right to the trailhead at **7.0** miles.

Going Farther

You can combine this with the Beaver and Buttonhook Bay Loops (Hike 61) for a 13.8-mile hike, or follow the 10-mile Buggy Trail loop around the north side of the park. ■

63. North Chilco Peak

RATING	DISTANCE	HIKING TIME
★★★★☆	4.2 miles round-trip	2.5 hours
ELEVATION GAIN	HIGH POINT	DIFFICULTY
1,525 feet	5,635 feet	◆◆◆◇
BEST MONTHS		
Jan Feb Mar Apr May **Jun Jul Aug Sep** Oct Nov Dec		

The Hike

Climb a National Recreational Trail to a rocky summit that serves up splendid territorial views while providing a strenuous workout.

Getting There

Take exit 12 from Interstate 90 and drive north on US Route 95 for about 15 miles to the Bunco Road exit to Silverwood Theme Park. Turn right on East Bunco Road (Forest Road 332), and drive about 2.3 miles where Bunco turns left. Follow Bunco for a mile and turn right. Drive 2.2 miles past a large parking area on the right, where the road begins to climb and turns to gravel. Continue uphill on FR 332 for 7.6 miles to the junction of FR 332 and FR 385. The trailhead, 4,128 feet above sea level, is on the right.

Spokane hikers wishing to avoid traffic in Coeur d'Alene and Hayden can take exit 7 from I-90 east of Post Falls and drive north on State Route 41 to Boekel Road. Turn right and follow Boekel to its junction with US 95 north of Hayden, then continue with the directions on the previous page.

The Trail

This hike begins on Chilco Mountain Recreational Trail 14 with a gentle climb above the road, then begins a series of nine short switchbacks in forest up a wide ridge where other hikers above could hear

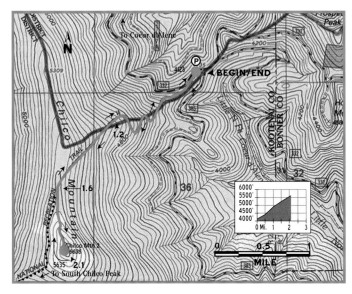

PERMITS/CONTACT
None required/Idaho Panhandle National Forest, (208) 664-2318, www.fs.usda.gov/ipnf

MAPS
USGS Athol

TRAIL NOTES
Leashed dogs OK

The North Chilco Peak Trail climbs out of the timber near the summit

me sweating and complaining about the steep grade, which continues steadily for a mile and 1,000 vertical feet. At **1.2** miles, it appears as if the trail crew gave up on the switchbacks and simply aimed to the southwest for the crest of the ridge below North Chilco Peak.

You'll reach that point in another 0.4 mile and 400 vertical feet, where I stopped bitching about the grade because I was out of breath. At **1.6** miles, the route actually flattens enough to pass a campsite and reaches a junction with the North Chilco Peak Trail. Turn left and ascend the north ridge of the mountain, first through alpine meadow and then climbing flat chunks of granite to the summit, **2.1** miles from the trailhead. Concrete foundation blocks are all that remain of a fire lookout built in the 1930s.

Going Farther
Hardbodies seeking more exercise can scramble down the southwest ridge of North Chilco or follow the trail back to Chilco Mountain Recreational Trail 14 and turn left, following it 2 miles to South Chilco Mountain, a higher peak by about 50 feet but without the grand vistas of the north peak. ■

64. Mineral Point

RATING	DISTANCE	HIKING TIME
★★★☆☆	4.5 miles round-trip	2.5 hours

ELEVATION GAIN	HIGH POINT	DIFFICULTY
240 feet	2,560 feet	◆◆◇◇◇

BEST MONTHS											
Jan	Feb	Mar	Apr	**May**	**Jun**	**Jul**	**Aug**	**Sep**	Oct	Nov	Dec

The Hike

This mostly downhill walk is the perfect way to warm up before a swim in Lake Pend Oreille's Green Bay, then get all sweaty on the climb back to the trailhead.

Getting There

Follow US Route 95 south from the Sandpoint Bypass for 6 miles to Sagle Road and turn left. Follow Sagle Road for 9 miles to Garfield Bay, passing the Garfield Bay boat launch and campground road for 0.2 mile along a lakefront park. Just past the park, turn left and drive another 0.3 mile to Mineral Point Road (Forest Road 532) on the right. Turn right and follow FR 532 for 2.8 miles, passing Green Bay Campground Road 2672 at 1.2 miles, to FR 532A and turn right to the trailhead, 2,560 feet above sea level. Restrooms are available.

PERMITS/CONTACT
None required/Idaho Panhandle National Forest,
(208) 263-5111, www.fs.usda.gov/ipnf

MAPS
USGS Packsaddle NW; online Forest Service map

TRAIL NOTES
Leashed dogs OK; mountain bikes and equestrians welcome

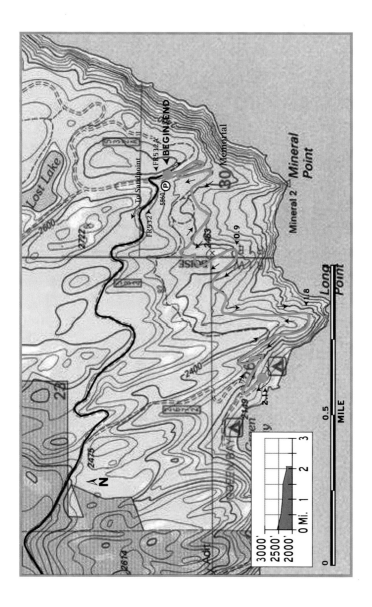

Lake Pend Oreille from the Mineral Point Trail

Spokane hikers wishing to avoid traffic in Coeur d'Alene and Hayden can take exit 7 from I-90 east of Post Falls and drive north on State Route 41 to Boekel Road. Turn right and follow Boekel to its junction with US 95 north of Hayden, then continue with the directions on page 228.

The Trail

We can all be thankful for this piece of the Idaho Panhandle National Forest and its Mineral Point Trail, since it contains a rare patch of public waterfront along gleaming Lake Pend Oreille. Boaters arrive to camp above the beaches at Green Bay and tent campers drive the bumpy FR 2672 down to join them. The Mineral Point Trail 82 drops from a forested ridge down to the campground, serving up spectacular views of the lake and colorful wildflower patches in the spring and early summer.

The path, built in 1989, drops steeply past an overlook and memorial to Brent K. "Jake" Jacobson, a US Forest Service officer who gave his life in service. The grade lessens after a couple of switchbacks and climbs a bit to a rock outcrop and view of the lake, **0.9** mile from the trailhead. From here, the trail traverses a forested gully and climbs to a second viewpoint above Long Point at **1.7** miles.

You'll find a bench and view in another 0.1 mile and begin dropping in forest to a junction with a trail leading downhill to the Green Bay Campground at **1.9** miles. Stay to the right and follow the trail to the campground parking area at **2.1** miles. Beyond, a nice beach along Green Bay beckons. This is your turnaround point.

Going Farther
By following trails and forest roads west from the trailhead, you can add a loop of more than 6 miles around the Lost Lake Trail 81. ■

65. Gold Hill Trail

RATING	DISTANCE	HIKING TIME
★★★☆☆	7.4 miles round-trip	4 hours
ELEVATION GAIN	**HIGH POINT**	**DIFFICULTY**
1,610 feet	3,743 feet	◆◆◆◇
BEST MONTHS		
Jan Feb Mar Apr **May Jun Jul Aug Sep** Oct Nov Dec		

The Hike
The views of Sandpoint and its Lake Pend Oreille and Selkirk Mountain setting don't get much better than this from viewpoints on a climb up 4,042-foot Gold Hill.

Getting There
From Sandpoint, follow US Route 95 south for 2 miles to Bottle Bay Road and turn left. Follow Bottle Bay for 4.8 miles to the trailhead on the right, 2,135 feet above sea level. A restroom is available.

Spokane hikers wishing to avoid traffic in Coeur d'Alene and Hayden can take exit 7 from I-90 east of Post Falls and drive north on State Route 41 to Boekel Road. Turn right and follow Boekel to

PERMITS/CONTACT
None required/Idaho Panhandle National Forest,
(208) 263-5111, www.fs.usda.gov/ipnf

MAPS
USGS Talache; online Forest Service map

TRAIL NOTES
Leashed dogs OK; mountain bikes and equestrians welcome

its junction with US 95 north of Hayden, then continue with the directions on the previous page.

The Trail

This hike is a no-nonsense climb to spectacular views of Lake Pend Oreille and the surrounding mountains. You'll appreciate the shade of the Idaho Panhandle National Forest on the seemingly endless switchbacks that take you to a forest road near the top of Gold Hill.

The path begins with thirty-nine switchbacks up a steep forested hillside, climbing more than 650 feet in 1.2 miles to round a ridge at

The view from the Gold Hill trail

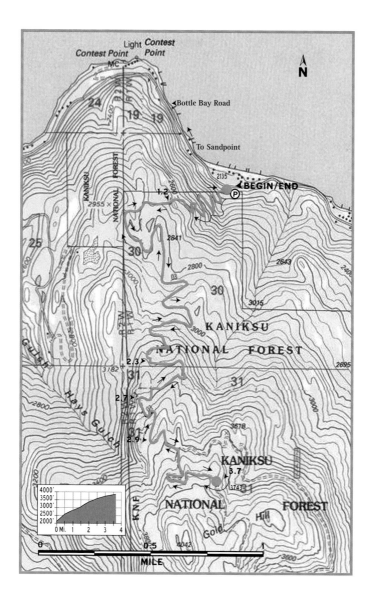

Contest Point
Light
Contest Point
MC
Contest Point

Bottle Bay Road

To Sandpoint

2135

BEGIN/END
P

1.2

2955 ×

2841

2800

3015

2643

2400

KANIKSU

NATIONAL FOREST

3000

2.3

3182

31

2695

2.7

2800

3678

2.9

3.7

1743

KANIKSU

NATIONAL FOREST

Gulch

Havs Gulch

KNF

NATIONAL   FOREST

Gold   Hill

4042

3800

3000

2200

4000'
3500'
3000'
2500'
2000'
0 Mi.   1   2   3   4

0   0.5   1
MILE

2,800 feet. Traverse into a deep forest and gully before climbing to the first viewpoint, **2.3** miles from the trailhead.

You'll round three more switchbacks to a second viewpoint with a couple of benches my ancient knees and lungs appreciated at **2.7** miles. The view includes downtown Sandpoint and the Long Bridge below (Hike 66).

At **2.9** miles, the trail emerges onto Forest Road 2642, an alternate trailhead on the north side of Gold Hill. Turn right on the road and follow it around a sharp switchback to the east, where views open through the forest to the northeast across the lake to the Cabinet Mountains. At **3.7** miles, you'll reach your turnaround point on the road.

Going Farther
You can follow FR 2642 to the left from the trail junction for more viewpoints for about 1.6 miles and a round-trip hike of 10.6 miles. ■

URBAN SANDPOINT

66. Sandpoint Long Bridge

RATING	DISTANCE	HIKING TIME
★★★★☆	4.6 miles round-trip	1.5 hours
ELEVATION GAIN	**HIGH POINT**	**DIFFICULTY**
40 feet	2,080 feet	◆◇◇◇◇
BEST MONTHS		
Jan Feb Mar Apr May Jun Jul Aug Sep Oct Nov Dec		

The Hike

This is a fine walk any time of the year for pedestrians, and an excellent tour for bicycles and wheelchairs on a paved bridge above the Pend Oreille River.

Getting There

Hikers from Coeur d'Alene can follow US Route 95 north to the City of Sandpoint exit for East Superior Street, turning right immediately into a parking lot at the Conoco gas station at the Serenity Lee Trailhead, 2,070 feet above sea level.

Spokane hikers wishing to avoid traffic in Coeur d'Alene and Hayden can take exit 7 from I-90 east of Post Falls and drive north on State Route 41 to Boekel Road. Turn right and follow Boekel to its junction with US 95 north of Hayden, then continue with the directions above.

PERMITS/CONTACT
None required/Sandpoint Online, www.sandpointonline.com

MAPS
USGS Sandpoint, USGS Sagle; online map

TRAIL NOTES
Leashed dogs OK; bikes welcome

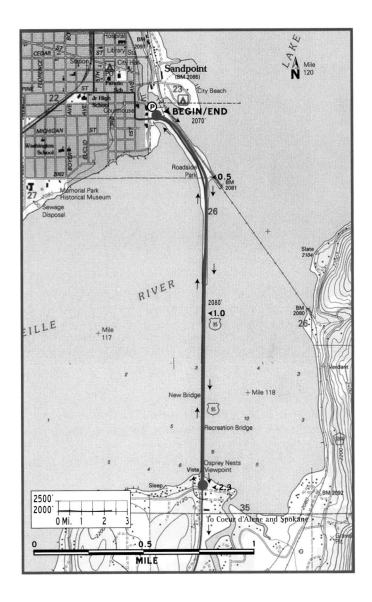

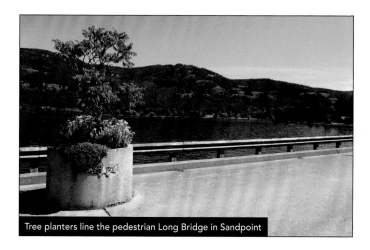
Tree planters line the pedestrian Long Bridge in Sandpoint

The Trail

The old highway bridge crossing the mouth of the Pend Oreille River today serves hundreds of walkers, wheelchair adventurers, and cyclists every year. It's popular with locals headed for a lunch-hour jog as well as families without a boat who want a day on the lake. Every August, the bridge serves as a grandstand for visitors watching the Long Bridge Swim, which annually attracts more than seven hundred swimmers.

The trail begins by ducking under the Sandpoint Bypass and turning south along the shore, first passing the Dog Beach Park. In addition to the sign advising visitors that Sandpoint is a "Walking Town," you should know that the city is very dog friendly. Past the dog beach, at about **0.5** mile, you'll climb to the old span, which parallels the 1981 US 95 bridge. If there's a downside to this hike, it's the noise from the highway.

At about **1.0** mile, cross above a well-used passage for boaters and note the tree planters decorated with mosaic fish and memorial plaques. Cate Huisman, writing in the *Sandpoint Reader*, tells the story of Sandpoint's Skip Pucci, who put the original trees and planters on the bridge.

Your turnaround point is at the south end of the bridge at Lakewood Avenue, **2.3** miles from the trailhead. The path continues beyond Lakewood, but becomes rough and crosses numerous roads and driveways.

Going Farther

The best way to make this a longer hike is to connect to the Pend d'Oreille Bay Trail (Hike 67). To do so, follow the path around the marina north to Bridge Street, cross toward the city park, and follow Sandpoint Avenue left to the trailhead. ■

67. Pend d'Oreille Bay Trail

RATING	DISTANCE	HIKING TIME
★★★★☆	3.0 miles round-trip	1.5 hours
ELEVATION GAIN	**HIGH POINT**	**DIFFICULTY**
30 feet	2,070 feet	◆◇◇◇◇

BEST MONTHS
Jan Feb Mar Apr May Jun Jul Aug Sep Oct Nov Dec

The Hike

The newest path around this neck of the woods is one of the best: a lakefront stroll that is in the city yet isolated from it by a railroad.

Getting There

Hikers from Coeur d'Alene can follow US Route 95 north to the City of Sandpoint exit for East Superior Street. Turn right and follow Superior to 1st Avenue and turn right. Follow 1st to Bridge Street and turn right, driving under the Sandpoint Bypass and railroad bridge to Dock Street. Turn left on Dock and follow it past the Edgewater Resort to Sandpoint Avenue and turn left. Follow Sandpoint Avenue past The Seasons at Sandpoint to the trailhead on the right, 2,070 feet above sea level. A portable toilet is available.

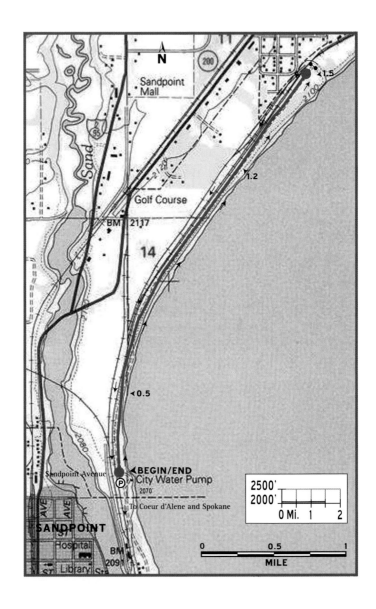

N

200

Sandpoint
Mall

95

2

Sand

2120

Golf Course

BM 2117

14

2100

1.5

1.2

0.5

◄BEGIN/END
City Water Pump

Sandpoint Avenue

(P)

2070'

To Coeur d'Alene and Spokane

2080

SANDPOINT

AVE

AVE

ST

Hospital

Library St.

BM
209'

2500'
2000'

0 Mi.   1   2

0   0.5   1
MILE

Spokane hikers wishing to avoid traffic in Coeur d'Alene and Hayden can take exit 7 from I-90 east of Post Falls and drive north on State Route 41 to Boekel Road. Turn right and follow Boekel to its junction with US 95 north of Hayden, then continue with the directions on page 239.

The Trail

We saved this hike for the winter to demonstrate that many of the hikes in this guide can be taken year-round. Some woodland pedestrians throughout the Inland Northwest stomp the snow to a hardpack surface and navigate them with traction devices. On the day we walked the Pend d'Oreille Bay Trail, a well-used solid pathway was easy to follow. Step off the track and you will sink in about 3 feet of snow.

The route begins at the city's water treatment plant and immediately drops to the rocky shoreline, rounding a point and leading north past old concrete blocks, decorated with graffiti, that may have been part of an old sawmill. The view of the Cabinet Mountains to the north and east is spectacular and probably best in the winter, when shoreline trees are leafless and the mountains are cloaked in white.

Pass a "Cairn of Thanks" at about **0.5** mile, which notes many of the families and individuals who helped create the trail. Volunteers and members of the Friends of the Pend d'Oreille Bay Trail as well as the cities of Sandpoint, Ponderay, and Kootenai maintain the route and plan to extend it in their communities. At around **1.2** miles, you'll see a sign explaining that this was once the site of the Panhandle Smelting and Refining Company, and that high levels of lead have been found in the soil and in the old slag heap that contains "black rock."

The route continues another 0.3 mile to a gate marking the current end of the trail and your turnaround point. Beyond is private property.

Going Farther

The best way to extend this hike is to return to the trailhead and follow Sandpoint Avenue back to Bridge Street, then take the Sandpoint Byway Trail north along Sand Creek for up to 2 miles one-way. Or combine this trail with that of Sandpoint Long Bridge (Hike 66). ∎

68. Mickinnick Trail

RATING	DISTANCE	HIKING TIME
★★★★☆	6.4 miles round-trip	4 hours
ELEVATION GAIN	HIGH POINT	DIFFICULTY
2,275 feet	4,310 feet	◆◆◆◇
	BEST MONTHS	
Jan Feb Mar Apr **May Jun Jul Aug Sep Oct** Nov Dec		

The Hike

Arguably one of the best urban hikes in the Inland Northwest, the Mickinnick Trail 13 takes you to lake and mountain vistas of many of the hikes around Sandpoint.

Getting There

From the Sandpoint Bypass, follow US Route 95 north to Schweitzer Cutoff Road and turn left. Drive 0.5 mile to North Boyer Road and turn right, following Boyer for 0.8 mile to Schweitzer Mountain Road. Turn left and drive 0.5 mile to Woodland Drive and turn left. Follow Woodland for 0.7 mile to the city park and trailhead on the right, 2,217 feet above sea level. A restroom is available at the trailhead.

Spokane hikers wishing to avoid traffic in Coeur d'Alene and Hayden can take exit 7 from I-90 east of Post Falls and drive north on State Route 41 to Boekel Road. Turn right and follow Boekel to its junction with US 95 north of Hayden, then continue with the directions on the opposite page.

The Trail

We both thanked and cursed Mick and Nicky Pleass, who donated 160 acres to the US Forest Service to make the Mickinnick Trail a reality. The thanks was for the awesome woodland trail—and to the volunteers, Forest Service, and City of Sandpoint, who built it—so close to the excellent food and beverage at Eichardt's Pub; the cursing (mostly mine) was for the steep grade of the path and at an old man's creaky knees.

The trail name is a combination of Mick, Nicky, and kinnikinnick, that shiny-leaved groundcover found beside many Inland Northwest

The view of Sandpoint and Lake Pend Oreille from the Mickinnick Trail

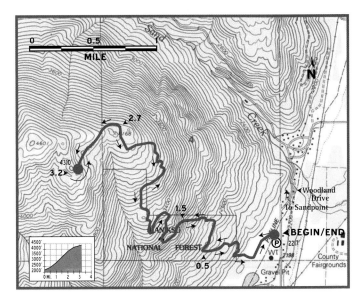

pathways. Walk across the flat city park to a gate marking the forest boundary and enter a mostly pine forest whose shade you'll appreciate on a hot summer day. The path begins climbing in switchbacks immediately, arriving at the first of several viewpoints and a bench **0.5** mile from the trailhead.

The grade eases a bit on a traverse before turning uphill again and climbing to a second bench and overlook at **1.5** miles. Here the route switches back and begins a gentler traverse to the south for about a quarter-mile.

Welcome the gentler grade because the next mile is a series of steep switchbacks that climb more than 650 feet around a 4,168-foot ridge before making a climbing traverse to the best view of all at **3.2** miles. You'll find several benches here, placed in memory of the Pleasses. I'm certain that all you young whippersnappers will have nothing but thanks for the folks to whom we owe this trail. ■

SANDPOINT NORTHEAST

69. Trestle Peak

RATING	DISTANCE	HIKING TIME
★★★☆☆	6.4 miles round-trip	3.5 hours
ELEVATION GAIN	**HIGH POINT**	**DIFFICULTY**
1,350 feet	6,320 feet	◆◆◆◇◇

BEST MONTHS
Jan Feb Mar Apr May **Jun Jul Aug Sep** Oct Nov Dec

The Hike

Here's a good huckleberry hike with nice views of the surrounding mountains, Trestle Creek valley, and Lake Pend Oreille.

Getting There

From the Sandpoint Bypass (US Route 95), drive north to State Route 200 and follow it east for 12 miles to Trestle Creek Road (Forest Road 275) and turn left. Follow this gravel road—a major forest thoroughfare to many mountain hikes—for 13 miles to a sharp hairpin and diverse camping spots. The trailhead, 4,990 feet above sea level, is on the left.

Spokane hikers wishing to avoid traffic in Coeur d'Alene and Hayden can take exit 7 from I-90 east of Post Falls and drive north on State Route 41 to Boekel Road. Turn right and follow Boekel to its junction with US 95 north of Hayden, then continue with the directions above from the Sandpoint Bypass.

PERMITS/CONTACT
None required/Idaho Panhandle National Forest,
(208) 263-5111, www.fs.usda.gov/ipnf

MAPS
USGS Mount Pend Oreille; online Forest Service map

TRAIL NOTES
Leashed dogs OK; mountain bikes and equestrians welcome;
be alert: this is grizzly country

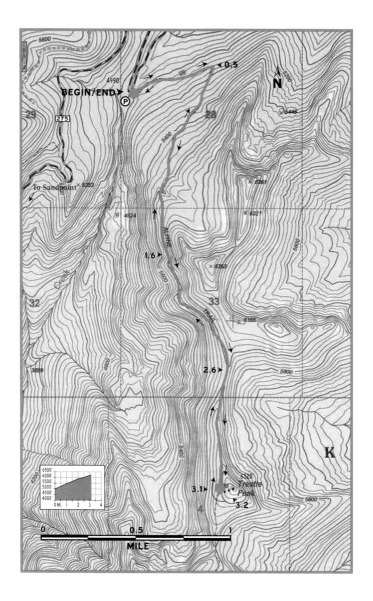

The Trestle Creek valley and Lake Pend Oreille from the Trestle Peak trail

The Trail

The Beetop-Round Top Trail 120 is a spectacular walk that follows the crest of mountains above Lake Pend Oreille for more than 10 miles, yielding views of the lake and surrounding mountains. This portion of the trail covers the first 3 miles of the northern end of the route. Because it's mostly along the ridge, water is scarce.

The trail climbs at a moderate pace for 0.5 mile in an evergreen forest where the understory is decorated by huckleberry bushes before switching back to the south, climbing more steeply, and then easing a bit, **1.2** miles from the trailhead.

At **1.6** miles, you'll traverse under a 6,353-foot peak and cross a talus slope where the views down the valley open to the east. Bear grass is showy in the early summer, before the huckleberries and mountain ash take over later. After traversing about a mile through alpine meadow views and forest, you'll reach a saddle below Trestle Peak, **2.6** miles from the trailhead.

The trail now climbs the sharp north ridge of the mountain, which is covered by heavy alpine timber, and passes under the west face of the summit at **3.1** miles. To gain a good view from the summit to the south and east, scramble through timber about 0.1 mile and 90 vertical feet. This is your turnaround point.

Going Farther

For a longer walk, the trail follows the ridge down and traverses under the east side for 1.5 miles to a 6,144-foot summit, making your hike a total of 9.4 miles. ■

70. Lake Darling

RATING	DISTANCE	HIKING TIME
★★★★	4.4 miles round-trip	3 hours

ELEVATION GAIN	HIGH POINT	DIFFICULTY
720 feet	5,280 feet	◆◆◆ ◇◇

BEST MONTHS
Jan Feb Mar Apr May Jun **Jul Aug Sep** Oct Nov Dec

The Hike

It would be difficult to find a better short, moderately difficult hike to a subalpine lake for huckleberry picking and a picnic.

Getting There

From the Sandpoint Bypass (US Route 95), drive north to State Route 200 and follow it east for 12 miles to Trestle Creek Road (Forest Road 275) and turn left. Follow this gravel road—a major forest thoroughfare to many mountain hikes—for 16 miles to Lightning Creek Road (FR 419). Turn left and follow the rougher FR 419 for about a mile to the trailhead on the left, just before crossing the Lightning Creek bridge, 4,570 feet above sea level.

Spokane hikers wishing to avoid traffic in Coeur d'Alene and Hayden can take exit 7 from I-90 east of Post Falls and drive north on State Route 41 to Boekel Road. Turn right and follow Boekel to its junction with US 95 north of Hayden, then continue with the directions above from the Sandpoint Bypass.

Lake Darling

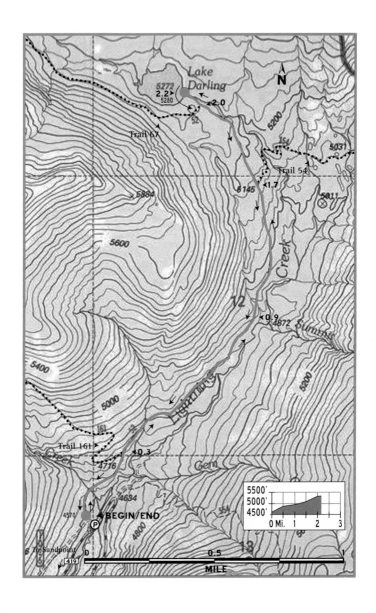

Lake Darling

5272
2.2►
5280
◄2.0

Trail 67

52

5200

5031

154
Trail 54

8145
◄1.7

5011
⊗

Creek

12

◄0.9
4872

Summit

5600

5884

5600

5400

5000

Hammond

Trail 161►

161

◄0.3

4776

Gem

4684

4570'

P ▲ BEGIN/END

4800

554

13

N

Elevation	
5500'	
5000'	
4500'	

0 Mi. 1 2 3

§ To Sandpoint

419

0

0.5

MILE

1

PERMITS/CONTACT
None required/Idaho Panhandle National Forest,
(208) 263-5111, www.fs.usda.gov/ipnf

MAPS
USGS Mount Pend Oreille; online Forest Service map

TRAIL NOTES
Leashed dogs OK; mountain bikes and equestrians welcome;
be alert: this is grizzly country

The Trail

This is a good introduction to the high lakes region of the Idaho Panhandle, where it's best to wait to visit until the hordes of bugs have gorged themselves on hikers and equestrians arriving earlier in the summer. You'll have plenty of company in the late summer, however, with huckleberry hunters clogging the trail and wrasslin' the griz for those delectable treats cooked up by Mother Nature.

Lake Darling Trail 52 climbs gently into the mixed evergreen forest to the northeast before traversing and crossing Gordon Creek to arrive at a junction with Gordon Creek Trail 161, **0.3** mile from the trailhead. Stay right and climb on a gentle grade above Lightning Creek, passing a streamside meadow at **0.9** mile.

Beyond, the route turns uphill to the north and begins climbing more steeply toward the lake. At **1.7** miles, keep left at the junction with Callahan Trail 54, and keep climbing to the lake basin ahead. Just before reaching the lake, cross the outlet at **2.0** miles where Trail 52 turns uphill around the west side of the lake. A grassy meadow on the east shore makes a good turnaround and picnic spot, **2.2** miles from the trailhead.

Going Farther

You can make an excellent high-ridge loop hike of about 7.5 miles by following Lake Darling Trail 52 uphill to the ridge south of Mount Pend Oreille, where you turn left on Pend Oreille Divide Trail 67 and follow it south for 1.3 miles to its junction with Gordon Creek Trail 161. Turn left and follow Gordon Creek Trail down to its junction with Lake Darling Trail, 0.3 mile from the trailhead. ■

71. Lake Estelle

RATING	DISTANCE	HIKING TIME
★★★★★	5.4 miles round-trip	3 hours

ELEVATION GAIN	HIGH POINT	DIFFICULTY
885 feet	5,770 feet	◆◆◆◇◇

BEST MONTHS
Jan Feb Mar Apr May **Jun Jul Aug Sep** Oct Nov Dec

The Hike

Pretty little Lake Estelle gleams in a granite cup in the Cabinet Mountains, a place of quiet solitude and serenity for wilderness pedestrians.

Getting There

From the Sandpoint Bypass (US Route 95), drive north to State Route 200 and follow it east for 12 miles to Trestle Creek Road (Forest Road 275) and turn left. Follow this gravel road—a major forest thoroughfare to many mountain hikes—for 16 miles to the Lightning Creek Road (FR 419). Turn left and follow the rougher FR 419 for 1.5 miles to Moose Creek Road (FR 1022) and turn right. Drive 2 miles on bumpy Moose Creek Road to the trailhead, 4,911 feet above sea level, where a restroom is available.

Spokane hikers wishing to avoid traffic in Coeur d'Alene and Hayden can take exit 7 from I-90 east of Post Falls and drive north on State Route 41 to Boekel Road. Turn right and follow Boekel to its

---

PERMITS/CONTACT
None required/Idaho Panhandle National Forest,
(208) 263-5111, www.fs.usda.gov/ipnf

MAPS
USGS Mount Pend Oreille; online Forest Service map

TRAIL NOTES
Leashed dogs OK; equestrians welcome; be alert: this is grizzly country

---

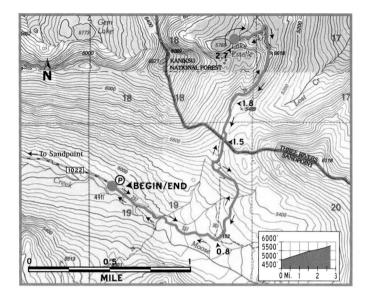

junction with US 95 north of Hayden, then continue with the directions on the facing page from the Sandpoint Bypass.

The Trail

Popular with backpackers and equestrians who enjoy established campsites at the trailhead and Moose Lake, the branch trail to Lake Estelle appears more lightly trod. In the late summer, the lower path is crowded with huckleberry hounds, but they seldom get as far as the lake. They fill their buckets on the first 200 yards of the trail and there's little point in walking farther. All the better for you, because the berries don't diminish and supply sweet energy for the moderate grade.

The trail climbs along Moose Creek for 0.2 mile to a junction with a trail leading to Blacktail Lake. Stay to the left on Moose Lake Trail 237 and climb another 0.6 mile to the junction with Lake Estelle Trail 36. Turn left here and begin a steeper climb through open timber slopes to a wide saddle on the ridge dividing the Moose Creek and Lost

Steep mountainside along the trail to Lake Estelle

Creek drainages at **1.5** miles. Meadows here are decorated with bear grass and wildflowers in early summer.

The trail begins a long climbing traverse on a steep hillside above the infant Lost Creek, rounding a cliff and rock sentinel **1.8** miles from the trailhead. The route then drops a bit to navigate below a granite sidehill at **2.2** miles, then switches back and climbs steeply to the lake at **2.7** miles. Time to hunker down, enjoy the peace and quiet, and let those huckleberries settle before turning around.

Going Farther

If you are comfortable scrambling off trail, circle Lake Estelle to the south and climb to the obvious saddle in the ridge to the west. It's about a half-mile to the saddle and another 600 vertical feet from the lake, but you'll get grand views and relative freedom from bugs in early summer and fall.

A longer option for those with two cars or who don't mind a 2.5-mile road walk is to continue west from the saddle, navigating steep slopes down to Gem Lake at about 0.6 mile, then following Gem Lake Trail 554 down to FR 1022. ■

72. Moose Mountain Loop

RATING	DISTANCE	HIKING TIME
★ ★ ★ ★ ★	7.6 miles round-trip	5 hours

ELEVATION GAIN	HIGH POINT	DIFFICULTY
2,100 feet	6,543 feet	♦ ♦ ♦ ♦ ◇

BEST MONTHS
Jan Feb Mar Apr May **Jun Jul Aug Sep** Oct Nov Dec

The Hike

This prime loop trek takes you from subalpine forest to high peaks, passing two alpine lakes along the way. Warning: Your pace will be slowed by huckleberry fields forever.

Getting There

From the Sandpoint Bypass (US Route 95), drive north to State Route 200 and follow it east for 12 miles to Trestle Creek Road (Forest Road 275) and turn left. Follow this gravel road—a major forest thoroughfare to many mountain hikes—for 16 miles to the Lightning Creek Road (FR 419). Turn left and follow the rougher FR 419 for 1.5 miles to Moose Creek Road (FR 1022) and turn right. Drive 2 miles on bumpy Moose Creek Road to the trailhead, 4,911 feet above sea level, where a restroom is available.

Spokane hikers wishing to avoid traffic in Coeur d'Alene and Hayden can take exit 7 from I-90 east of Post Falls and drive north on State Route 41 to Boekel Road. Turn right and follow Boekel to

---

PERMITS/CONTACT
None required/Idaho Panhandle National Forest,
(208) 263-5111, www.fs.usda.gov/ipnf

MAPS
USGS Mount Pend Oreille; online Forest Service map

TRAIL NOTES
Leashed dogs OK; equestrians welcome; be alert: this is grizzly country

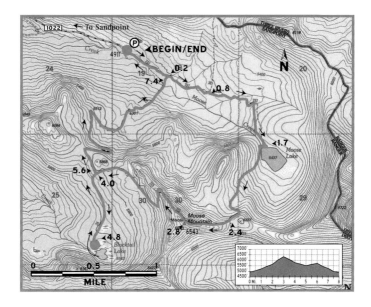

its junction with US 95 north of Hayden, then continue with the directions from the Sandpoint Bypass on the previous page.

The Trail

Popular with backpackers and equestrians who enjoy established campsites at the trailhead and Moose Lake, this route makes an excellent day hike for those who wish to travel light. If you take this walk in mid- to late August, you won't be traveling light, thanks to all the huckleberries you'll eat. You can get purple hands faster than you can say "yummy."

The trail climbs along Moose Creek for 0.2 mile to a junction with your return trail from Blacktail Lake. Stay to the left on Moose Lake Trail 237 and climb another 0.6 mile to the junction with Lake Estelle Trail 36. Keep right here and continue climbing through a thick understory of huckleberry bushes. The way steepens a bit the last half-mile before reaching pretty Moose Lake, **1.7** miles from the trailhead.

To continue, cross Moose Creek and follow the eastern shore on Moose Mountain Trail 213 as it climbs steeply, then very steeply, in subalpine forest and finally rocky cliffside to the western ridge of Moose Mountain at **2.4** miles. The trail ascends directly up the open ridge, with views of the surrounding mountains in every direction. You'll reach the

Moose Lake

6,543-foot summit of Moose Mountain at **2.8** miles.

Next, descend the ridge to the northwest, switching back into forest above the Blacktail Lake basin. At **4.0** miles, arrive at the junction with Blacktail Lake Trail 24. If you wish to shorten your hike by 1.6 miles, turn right and follow the trail back to the parking area. Though I was shuffling along like a trail slug and sweating streams large enough for trout migration, we chose to visit Blacktail Lake and turned left here.

It proved to be worth my fatigue because Blacktail Lake, **4.8** miles from the trailhead, is a dazzling alpine gem set in a rocky cirque. It's also a great rest stop and high enough, at 5,542 feet, to discourage bugs in late summer. After a rest, we turned around and traversed back to the Moose Mountain Trail junction, stayed left, and descended the trail to close the loop at **7.4** miles. Turn left to reach the trailhead.

Going Farther

Though it's difficult to imagine anyone other than a Forest Service smokejumper or hotshot firefighter with the energy to do it, you can add another 4 miles to this hike by taking the trail to Lake Estelle (Hike 71). ■

73. Harrison Lake

RATING	DISTANCE	HIKING TIME
★★★★★	4.8 miles round-trip	3 hours

ELEVATION GAIN	HIGH POINT	DIFFICULTY
1,400 feet	6,190 feet	◆◆◆◇◇

BEST MONTHS
Jan Feb Mar Apr May **Jun Jul Aug Sep** Oct Nov Dec

The Hike

The steep climb to this splendid alpine lake under the Selkirk Crest is well worth the effort, a popular trail with backpackers and day hikers alike.

Getting There

Drive north on the Sandpoint Bypass (US Route 95) for 13 miles to Pack River Road (Forest Road 231) and turn left. Follow Pack River Road for 20 miles to the trailhead with a restroom, 4,746 feet above sea level.

Spokane hikers wishing to avoid traffic in Coeur d'Alene and Hayden can take exit 7 from I-90 east of Post Falls and drive north on State Route 41 to Boekel Road. Turn right and follow Boekel to its junction with US 95 north of Hayden, then continue with the directions above from the Sandpoint Bypass.

PERMITS/CONTACT
None required/Idaho Panhandle National Forest,
(208) 263-5111, www.fs.usda.gov/ipnf

MAPS
USGS The Wigwams; online Forest Service map

TRAIL NOTES
Leashed dogs OK; be alert: this is grizzly country

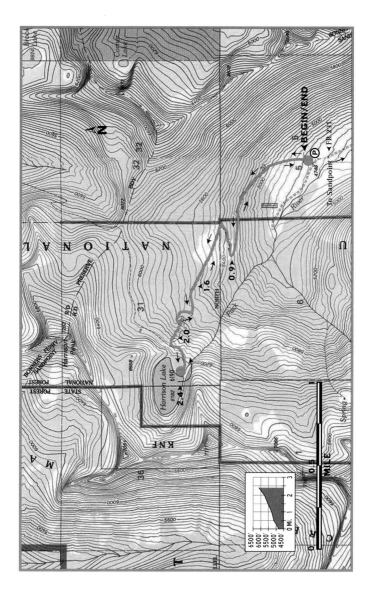

Harrison Lake

The Trail

Here we were reminded of some of the hikes we've taken in the North Cascades and Canadian Rockies, surrounded by—and climbing up—glacier-polished granite. The path, Trail 217, is easily followed and looks as if the first half-mile or so was once a double-track four-wheel-drive route. The path crosses several sections of granite but will probably be marked by rock cairns. If in doubt, climb west-northwesterly, keeping the infant Pack River on your left.

The first half-mile of the path is open and affords a view to the south of the Beehive Dome, a giant pile of granite smoothed by an ancient glacier. You'll soon enter an alpine forest with only tree-ka-boo views of the surroundings before arriving at a switchback **0.9** mile from the trailhead.

Beyond, the trail switches back again and climbs into an alpine meadow dotted with fir, where the trail has been tromped deep by herds of hikers headed to the lake. At **1.6** miles, the grade eases a bit for a short traverse, then turns uphill steeply, crossing open granite slabs to a junction, **2.0** miles from the trailhead, with a trail leading down to Murtle Creek.

This junction caused a mildly heated discussion with my wife, B. B. Hardbody, who insisted we turn left. I was absolutely certain we should turn right. Trail signs at the junction might have been better placed, I reasoned. "Fuzzbrain," opined B. B., "we go left." I prevailed. After all, I am a professional. This resulted in walking an extra 1.5 miles before I was willing to admit that she was correct. Big deal.

Point being, go left at this junction. Climb on granite slabs for about 0.4 mile before the path enters the Harrison Lake cirque, a beautiful rocky bowl underneath 7,292-foot Harrison Peak to the north.

Going Farther

You can add another 1.4 miles round-trip to this hike by following the western shore around the lake and scrambling up talus and smooth granite to the ridge to the west of Harrison Peak. The mountain panorama from here is unbeatable. ■

74. The Green Monarch

RATING	DISTANCE	HIKING TIME
★☆☆☆☆	6.2 miles round-trip	4 hours
ELEVATION GAIN	**HIGH POINT**	**DIFFICULTY**
1,780 feet	5,076 feet	♦ ♦ ♦ ♦
BEST MONTHS		
Jan Feb Mar Apr **May Jun Jul Aug Sep** Oct Nov Dec		

The Hike

Climb and descend and climb again in forest above Lake Pend Oreille to an evergreen-cloaked peak with an enchanting name and, at the end, a panoramic view.

Getting There

From the Sandpoint Bypass (US Route 95), drive north to State Route 200 and follow it east for 25 miles to Stevens Street in Clark Fork. Turn right on Stevens and cross the bridge, then take the first right. Drive 1.1 miles, passing a boat launch, to gravel Johnson Creek Road (Forest Road 278). Follow Johnson Creek Road for 7 miles to where

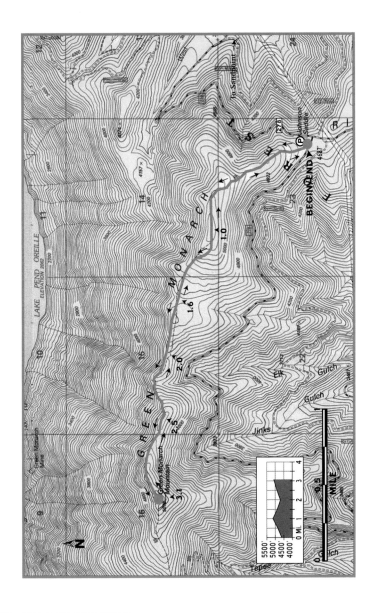

PERMITS/CONTACT
None required/Idaho Panhandle National Forest,
(208) 263-5111, www.fs.usda.gov/ipnf

MAPS
USGS Packsaddle Mountain; online Forest Service map

TRAIL NOTES
Leashed dogs OK; mountain bikes, dirt bikes, and equestrians welcome

it turns right. Follow it right and immediately right again into the trailhead parking area, 4,687 feet above sea level.

Spokane hikers wishing to avoid traffic in Coeur d'Alene and Hayden can take exit 7 from I-90 east of Post Falls and drive north on State Route 41 to Boekel Road. Turn right and follow Boekel to its junction with US 95 north of Hayden, then continue with the directions from the Sandpoint Bypass on page 261.

The Trail

This is a long drive for Spokane and Coeur d'Alene hikers, but if you have the time, don't miss this forest walk to one of the emerald mountains that hunkers above the wild south shore of Lake Pend Oreille. I admit it: I chose this hike because of its poetic name and by reading glowing accounts by other hikers.

Wilderness pedestrians who don't mind sharing the trail with dirt bikes are likely to enjoy this route more. We didn't encounter any on our hike in August 2016, but evidence of motorized use on the trail was obvious by the several inches of dust on the path and steep gouges around switchbacks. Parts of this route are very steep and nicely suited for motorbikes only; the trail is closed to all-terrain vehicles and motorized vehicles over 50 inches wide.

The Green Monarch Trail 69 begins climbing immediately, first on a wide, gentle grade bordered by scrub pine. After about a quarter-mile, the route steepens and enters a more mature stand of evergreens, climbing to the 5,140-foot-high crest of the Green Monarch ridge at **1.0** mile. Lake Pend Oreille glimmers through the trees less

The trail to the Green Monarch

than a mile to the north and 3,000 feet below.

You'll traverse for less than 0.1 mile, then descend steeply to the first of four timbered saddles on the ridge, **1.6** miles from the trailhead. Climb over an 80-foot hump in the ridge, then descend steeply to a second saddle at **2.0** miles. The route begins climbing immediately, then drops in a very steep switchback to another saddle.

The thick forest here interrupts views of the lake and surrounding country, and you'll cross a bench and begin a final descent to a saddle, then climb directly up a sharp ridge to the false summit of Green Monarch Mountain at **2.5** miles. This yields the best views of the lake and Cabinet, Selkirk, and Bitterroot Mountains to the north, east, and west. The final half-mile of the climb leads to the 5,076-foot summit of the Green Monarch, your turnaround point.

Going Farther

It's another 3.2 round-trip miles and 1,080 vertical feet to 5,219-foot Schafer Peak, making the total distance 9.4 miles. The trail drops to a junction with the Teepee Gulch Trail 105 after 0.6 mile at 4,600 feet before climbing up a sharp ridge to the summit. ■

75. Scotchman Peak

RATING	DISTANCE	HIKING TIME
★ ★ ★ ★ ★	8.4 miles round-trip	5.5 hours

ELEVATION GAIN	HIGH POINT	DIFFICULTY
3,740 feet	7,009 feet	♦ ♦ ♦ ♦ ♦

BEST MONTHS
Jan Feb Mar Apr May **Jun Jul Aug Sep** Oct Nov Dec

The Hike

Many wilderness pedestrians consider this to be the ultimate hike in the Inland Northwest, and with good reason. The vistas are unbeatable, the workout is exhausting, and the mountain goats are often a nuisance.

Getting There

From the Sandpoint Bypass (US Route 95), drive north to State Route 200 and follow it east for 25 miles to Clark Fork. Turn left on Lightning Creek Road and drive 1.2 miles, keeping left past the University of Idaho Clark Fork campus on Mosquito Creek Road (Forest Road 276), to the junction with FR 2295. Turn right and drive 1 mile to FR 2294, turn left, and follow it to FR 2294A. Turn left here and follow FR 2294A to the trailhead, 3,302 feet above sea level. Signs directing drivers to Scotchman Peak Trail 65 are posted at most of the road junctions.

PERMITS/CONTACT
None required/Idaho Panhandle National Forest,
(208) 263-5111, www.fs.usda.gov/ipnf; Friends of Scotchman
Peaks Wilderness, www.scotchmanpeaks.org

MAPS
USGS Scotchman Peak; online Forest Service map

TRAIL NOTES
Leashed dogs OK; equestrians welcome

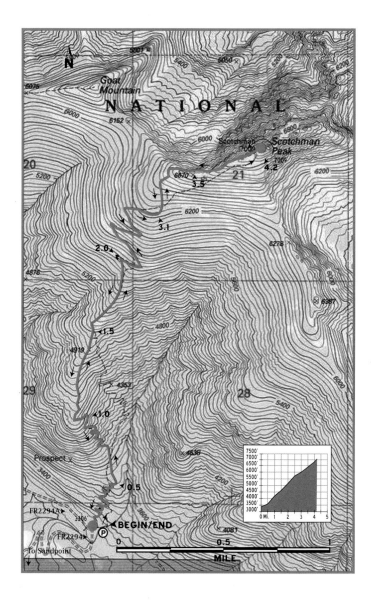

N

Goat
Mountain

N A T I O N A L

Scotchman
7066

Scotchman
Peak
7009'
4.2

3.5

3.1

2.0

1.5

1.0

0.5

Prospect

FR2294A

FR2294

To Sandpoint

BEGIN/END

P

0   0.5   1
MILE

The trail near the summit of Scotchman Peak

Spokane hikers wishing to avoid traffic in Coeur d'Alene and Hayden can take exit 7 from I-90 east of Post Falls and drive north on State Route 41 to Boekel Road. Turn right and follow Boekel to its junction with US 95 north of Hayden, then continue with the directions from the Sandpoint Bypass on page 265.

The Trail

The climb to the summit of Scotchman Peak is unrelenting from beginning to end, although you will have opportunities to catch your breath on several long traverses where the grade eases a bit. Volunteers have done a commendable job of rerouting the trail in spots to make a more comfortable climb, and markers we found when we visited in August 2016 indicated that more work was planned.

The organization, Friends of Scotchman Peaks Wilderness, provides guided hikes here and stages various activities in support of trails throughout the proposed wilderness area. The group is an excellent resource for hiking throughout the Inland Northwest and provides volunteers to help hikers understand mountain goat behavior along this trail.

Before getting started, be sure you're carrying water; there's none along the way. Begin by climbing a series of short switchbacks on newer trail for 0.5 mile, then turning directly uphill for another 0.5 mile. This section was scheduled for rerouting as this guide was being published. You'll switchback at **1.5** miles, then climb steadily for another 0.5 mile, turning directly up a forested ridge. Until this point, hikers have the benefit of some forest shade.

At around **2.0** miles, the path breaks into "The Meadows," where alpine evergreens provide scant shade and the views begin to rejuvenate old guys like me who gain a second wind in mountains near timberline. The grade eases a bit to scale a wide ridge in a half-dozen switchbacks, **3.1** miles from the trailhead.

Then the grade becomes steeper again, climbing 400 vertical feet in 0.4 mile to the west ridge of Scotchman Peak. Mountain goats are commonly seen along this section of trail and cooling off on the long-lingering snow in the steep bowl to the north. You'll climb on rock over a false summit along the ridge, finally reaching the true summit at **4.2** miles.

Grab the champagne. Fist-bump. Rest your knees for the downhill grind. ■

RESOURCES

Outdoors Clubs and Volunteer Opportunities

The Backpacking Club, www.backpackingclub.macwebsitebuilder.com

Friends of Mount Spokane State Park, www.mountspokane.org

Friends of the Pend d'Oreille Bay Trail, www.pobtrail.org

Friends of Scotchman Peaks Wilderness, www.scotchmanpeaks.org

Inland Northwest Hikers (including the Hobnailers, Inc.), www.meetup .com/Inland-Northwest-Hikers

Inland Northwest Trails Coalition, www.facebook.com/inland-northwest -trails-coalition-18558514966

Ms. Adventures of the Inland Northwest, www.meetup.com /ms-adventures-of-the-inland-northwest

North Idaho Adventurers Club, www.meetup.com/adventurers-327

Panhandle Nordic Club, www.panhandlenordicclub.com

Spokane Mountaineers, www.spokanemountaineers.org

Spokane Nordic Ski Association, www.spokanenordic.org

Pamphlets

North Idaho Trail Guide, Upper Columbia River Sierra Club pamphlet, $7

Spokane Trail Guide #1, Upper Columbia River Sierra Club pamphlet, $7

Spokane Trail Guide #2, Upper Columbia River Sierra Club pamphlet, $7

Sandpoint Ranger District Trails, Idaho Panhandle National Forest pamphlet, free

INDEX

ABOUT THE AUTHOR

As a youngster in Spokane, Washington, **SEABURY BLAIR JR.** hiked—often lost—around the hills of his native city. He continues to get lost (though with far greater skill) after six decades of practice, on trails from the Olympic Peninsula to Glacier National Park.

A freelance Pacific Northwest travel writer and outdoor columnist for the *Bremerton Sun* for more than seventeen years, Blair emphatically denies that the paper changed its name to the *Kitsap Sun* in order to disassociate itself from him. He is the recipient of national writing awards from Scripps Howard and Associated Press Sports Editors.

Blair is the author of *Backcountry Ski! Washington*, *Day Hike! Columbia Gorge*, *Day Hike! Olympic Peninsula*, *The Creaky Knees Guide Washington*, *The Creaky Knees Guide Oregon*, *The Creaky Knees Guide Northwest National Parks and Monuments*, and *Wild Roads Washington*.